What Is at Stake in Building "Non-Western" International Relations Theory?

T0299996

International Relations (IR) as a discipline is often deemed to be "too Western" centric. It has been argued that much of mainstream IR theory is "simply an abstraction of Western history." In this respect, many IR scholars have called for "broadening" the theoretical horizon of IR while problematising the Western parochialism of the discipline, and it is increasingly acknowledged that IR needs to embrace a wider range of histories, experiences, and theoretical perspectives, particularly those outside of the West. However, despite such a meaningful debate over broadening the theoretical and practical horizons of IR, several critical questions remain unclear and under-explored. For example, does IR need to embrace pluralism? If so, how much? To what extent, and in what sense, is IR parochial? Should IR promote dialogue across theoretical and spatial divides? If so, how? Yong-Soo Eun addresses these questions. He undertakes a literature review and an empirical analysis of the extent to which the field has actually become diverse and pluralistic. This investigation considers diversity beyond the current limited focus on the geographical origins of theory. Yong-Soo also draws attention to the mechanisms and processes of knowledge production and transmission in IR. More importantly, he addresses what is probably the most acute issue associated with the "non-Western" IR theory-building enterprise; namely, fragmentation and dialogue. In conclusion, Yong-Soo notes that the role of unsettling the present hierarchical structure of the discipline falls to reflexive individual agents. He argues that in order for their agential power to be more fully harnessed in the opening up of IR, critical "self"-reflection and "collective" empathy and collaboration among marginalised scholars are all essential.

Yong-Soo Eun is Associate Professor of Political Science and International Studies at Hanyang University (HYU), Seoul. Before joining HYU, he taught at the University of Warwick in the UK. He has published articles in scholarly journals, including *Review of International Studies*, *International Studies Perspectives*, and *PS: Political Science and Politics*. Yong-Soo is broadly interested in IR theory and the international politics of the Asia-Pacific region.

IR Theory and Practice in Asia

This series will publish philosophical, theoretical, methodological and empirical work by prominent scholars, as well as that of emerging scholars, concerned with IR theory and practice in the context of Asia. It will engage with a wide range of issues and questions ranging from meta-theoretical underpinnings of existing Western-oriented IR theories to ways of theorising Asian histories and cultures.

For a full list of titles in this series, please visit: www.routledge.com/IR-Theory-and-Practice-in-Asia/book-series/IRTPA

What Is at Stake in Building "Non-Western" International Relations Theory?

Yong-Soo Eun

Routledge
Taylor & Francis Group

LONDON AND NEW YORK

First published 2018 by Routledge

2 Park Square, Milton Park, Abingdon, Oxfordshire OX14 4RN
52 Vanderbilt Avenue, New York, NY 10017

Routledge is an imprint of the Taylor & Francis Group, an informa business

First issued in paperback 2019

British Library Cataloguing in Publication Data
A catalogue record for this book is available from the British Library

Library of Congress Cataloging in Publication Data
Names: Eun, Yong-Soo, author.
Title: What is at stake in building "non-western" international relations theory? / Yong-Soo Eun.
Description: Abingdon, Oxon ; New York, NY : Routledge, 2018. | Series: IR theory and practice in Asia ; 2 | Includes bibliographical references and index.
Identifiers: LCCN 2017012122 | ISBN 9781138282544 (hardback) | ISBN 9781315270678 (ebook)
Subjects: LCSH: International relations--Philosophy. | East and West.
Classification: LCC JZ1305 .E88 2018 | DDC 327.101--dc23
LC record available at https://lccn.loc.gov/2017012122

ISBN: 978-1-138-28254-4 (hbk)
ISBN: 978-0-367-37564-5 (pbk)

Typeset in Times New Roman
by Taylor & Francis Books

To my beloved family

Contents

Tables

Acknowledgements and preface

What is at stake in building "non-Western" IR theory? This is a difficult question to answer, because it involves the fundamental issue of theory building and requires a firm grasp of the inner workings of a social science discipline; but it is for this very reason that the question is an important one. I am not sure if I have succeeded in my attempt to answer it. Although I am aware that the book may not offer clear answers, I hope that you will see this book as a worthwhile attempt that merits criticism and further investigation, and that it will stimulate you to think about these issues further.

I owe personal thanks and an intellectual debt to many people for the completion of this book. First of all, I must give hearty thanks to Shaun Breslin for his unstinting support and helpful comments on my studies and research projects. I also owe special thanks to Yaqing Qin, Tim Dunne, Alexander Wendt, Colin Wight, L. H. M. Ling, and T. V. Paul for their constructive feedback on my discussion about diversity and fragmentation in IR theory. This book has benefited immensely from the talks we have had and the comments and encouragement they have given me in various ways and on various occasions. In addition, I have attempted to make progress in understanding the issue of diversity in IR theory through building on and expanding the discussions and arguments of my earlier works (Eun 2016, for example) when I was writing this book. Nonetheless, new thoughts (especially on how to promote dialogue in IR) that I have recently developed thanks to a series of "dialogue" I have had with Patrick Jackson are not reflected in the manuscript (which was completed in early 2017). I am planning to publish a second version of this book with more updated and sophisticated discussions as soon as possible.

My sincere thanks must go to Simon Bates, Olivia Hatt, Maggie Reid, and ShengBin Tan at Routledge for their understanding, patience, and support for this book. I am also very grateful to Daniel Moure for his

Acknowledgements and preface

excellent editorial help. Thanks to their attention to detail, the stringency and clarity of the writing style have been improved. I gratefully acknowledge the financial support of the following institutions while this book was being planned and developed: Hanyang University and the National Research Foundation of Korea (NRF-2016S1A5A8020037). Finally, I express my deep gratitude to my beloved family (Eun Daeshik, Eun sunyoung, Jang byungchul, Chae-Yun, Jun-Hyeoc, Min-Jung, and Han Eun Soon) for everything.

"Much about coffee's flavour still remains a mystery," said Ted Lingle in his *Coffee Cupper's Handbook*. Although we do not know exactly how coffee's flavour emerges, we do know one thing: if we want to enjoy rich flavours of coffee, various types of beans and various ways of preparing and brewing them are both needed. The same is true of progress in IR. International studies should be undertaken not only from various regional standpoints, but also with various epistemologies and methodologies. I hope this book can contribute to enriching the ongoing "broadening" IR project, be it "non-Western," "post-Western," or "Global" IR, and thus help IR enjoy various flavours of knowing.

Yong-Soo Eun
Hanyang University, Seoul

1 Opening up the debate over "non-Western" International Relations

It is often pointed out that International Relations (IR)[1] as a discipline is "too Western-centric" (Tickner 2013; Acharya 2014, 2016) and that much of mainstream IR theory is "simply an abstraction of Western history" (Buzan 2016: 156; see also Carvalho et al. 2011; Hobson 2012; Ling 2014). In J. Ann Tickner's words, IR scholarship has long been focused on questions of "importance to the great powers of the Eurocentric Westphalian system" (Tickner 2016: 158). According to John Hobson (2012: 1), IR continues to seek "to parochially celebrate or defend or promote the West as the proactive subject of, and as the highest or ideal normative referent in, world politics." Put simply, IR "often marginalizes those outside … the West" (Acharya 2014: 647).

In this respect, many IR scholars have called for "broadening" the theoretical horizon of IR while problematising the Western parochialism of the discipline, and it is increasingly acknowledged that IR needs to embrace a wider range of histories, experiences, knowledge claims, and theoretical perspectives, particularly those outside of the West. In addition, calling for more diversity in IR theory and greater pluralism in the discipline is justified due to not only the under-representation (or marginalisation) of non-Western worlds in the theoretical study of international relations, but also the intrinsic complexity, variety, and contingency inherent in twenty-first-century global politics (Breslin 2007; Dunne et al. 2013b; Dunne et al. 2015; Paul 2016; Lake 2016). Of course, as will be discussed in detail in the following section, contemporary events such as the rise of China have contributed to the development of alternative (or indigenous) theoretical frameworks (Qin 2011, Qin 2016; Xuetong 2011; Zhang 2012).

Mapping the terrain of the ongoing debate over "non-Western" IR

In these contexts, whether there are any substantial merits to developing a "non-Western" IR theory and what such a theory would (or should) look like are topics of heated debate in contemporary IR. This interest in the theorisation of "non-Western" IR results largely from discontent with the epistemic value of mainstream theories – namely, realism, liberalism, and constructivism – all of which have "Western" or, more specifically, "Eurocentric" (Patomäki 2007) conceptual, analytical, and normative underpinnings (Johnston 2012: 53–55). Western/Eurocentric theories, the criticism goes, misrepresent and therefore misunderstand much of "the rest of the world" (Acharya 2014: 647). In addition, advocates of "non-Western" IR theory building often point out that Asia has cultures, institutions, norms, and world views that are inherently different from those derived from or advanced in Europe.

Long-standing interests and growing endorsement

Consider, for example, David Kang's critique. In his well-known piece "Getting Asia Wrong," Kang (2003: 57, 58) calls for "new analytical frameworks," noting that "most international relations theory … derived from the European experience of the past four centuries [...] do a poor job as they are applied to Asia." Critiques of this kind have long served as a starting premise in theoretical studies on Asian international relations. Almost two decades ago, Peter Katzenstein (1997: 5) writes as follows: "Theories based on Western, and especially West European, experience have been of little use in making sense of Asian regionalism." Similarly, Jeffrey Herbst (2000: 23) comments that "[i]nternational relations theory, derived from an extended series of case studies of Europe, has become notorious for falling short of accounting for the richness and particularity of Asia's regional politics." Amitav Acharya and Barry Buzan have made a similar argument in their edited volume, *Non-Western International Relations Theory*:

> The puzzle for us is that the sources of international relations theory conspicuously fail to correspond to the global distribution of its subjects. Our question is: "why is there no non-Western international theory?" We are as intrigued by the absence of theory in the non-West.
>
> (Acharya and Buzan 2010: 1)

Here, China's rise has added momentum to long-standing attempts to build new or indigenous theoretical frameworks – especially within the Chinese IR community. Yaqing Qin at the China Foreign Affairs University asserts that Chinese IR theory "is likely and even inevitable to emerge along with the great economic and social transformation that

China has been experiencing" (Qin 2007: 313). In a later piece on a similar topic, Qin explains why the development of a Chinese IR theory is "inevitable": the major achievements of the last three decades in the Chinese IR community have been made by "learning" Western IR; yet

> the more Chinese have learned, the more they want to create, especially when they find that Western IR theory is sometimes unable to provide satisfactory explanation. ... If persistent efforts are made, it will be inevitable for Chinese IR theory, with local experience and universal validity, to emerge and grow.
>
> (Qin 2011: 252–253)

It seems that the logic underlying this projection is associated not only with the observation that China is rising, but also with the political desire to advance the national interests of China. The scholarly practices of building an IR theory "with Chinese characteristics" are a case in point. For example, consider the arguments put forward by Shoude Liang at Beijing University. Liang is one of many Chinese scholars who argue for the need for an IR theory that reflects China's cultural traditions and national interests. Specifically, he suggests that Chinese scholars should bring "Chinese characteristics" to the fore in the study of international relations; going a step further, he emphasises that "the end purpose of IR" in China should be "to safeguard China's national sovereignty and to serve its national interest, and to ... carry on the historical tradition of Chinese culture" (Liang 1994: 18; see also Song 2001).

Indeed, this political approach to the use of theory does not appear to be unique to China. The notion that theory should serve as a tool for promoting national interests runs through the Korean IR community as well. According to Chun and Park (2002: 7), "Korean IR theory" needs to provide "guidelines for Korea's foreign policy actions" and to serve as "a political means of reflecting Korean voices in world politics" and enhancing "the status of Korean theorists in global IR scholarship." Similarly, Hahm (2008: 38) states that the "Korean School" of IR should be an "IR of Korea, by Korea, and for Korea." Kang (2003), Park (2005), and Yu and Park (2008) all promote a nationalist IR theory. As Yu and Park (2008: 57) argue, "the indigenization of IR" in Korea means the development of an IR theory and research methods based on Korea's experiences and instances; and "this should accord with the pursuit of Korea's national interests."

Of course, the end purpose of a "non-Western" IR theory could vary greatly, depending on how we make sense of what IR theory means and what it should do, but existing disagreements over the purpose of

IR theory do not impede the search for sources upon which an alternative IR theory can be built. Indeed, many IR scholars in non-Western countries have made considerable attempts to discern their nations' unique social ontologies or historical-cultural traditions in their quest to develop a "non-Western" IR; this is especially the case with Chinese IR. Confucianism, Marxism, *"Tianxia"* (天下, all-under-heaven), the Chinese tributary system (朝贡体制), and the philosophies of Mao Zedong and Deng Xiaoping are all cited as theoretical resources for Chinese IR (see, e.g., Song 2001; Qin 2007, 2011; Callahan 2008; Zhao 2009; Kang 2010; Wang 2011; Xuetong 2011; Wan 2012; Zhang 2012; Horesh 2013). Although consensus on what "Chinese characteristics" actually are has yet to be determined, many Chinese (and non-Chinese) scholars hold that the establishment of a Chinese IR theory is desirable or natural. In Qin's words (2011: 250)

> a general consensus among Chinese scholars was reached in the mid-1990s on the possibility and desirability of building Chinese IRT [IR theory], and the discussion since 2000 has focused more on how to build Chinese IRT than whether to develop Chinese IRT.

Going a step further, Peter Kristensen and Ras Nielsen claim that "the innovation of a Chinese IR theory is a *natural* product of China's geopolitical rise, its growing political ambitions, and discontent with Western hegemony" (Kristensen and Nielsen 2013: 19, emphasis added).

Criticisms

At the same time, a number of empirical, epistemological, and normative criticisms have been raised against attempts to develop a Chinese IR theory and (by extension) "non-Western" IR. Empirically, Asian international relations are not fundamentally different from those of Europe, in the sense that anarchy, survival, and the balance of power have been the key operating principles of state-to-state interactions since the pre-modern period. For example, based on a detailed archive analysis of China's foreign relations under the Song and Ming dynasties, Yuan-kang Wang concludes that in the "anarchical" international environment at that time, "Confucian culture did not constrain ... [Chinese] leaders' decisions to use force; in making such decisions, leaders have been mainly motivated by their assessment of the balance of power between China and its adversary" (Wang 2011: 181). This finding leads Wang to defend the theoretical utility of structural realism based on the Westphalian system.

Epistemologically, too, critics point out that it is "unscientific" to emphasise and/or incorporate a particular culture or the world view of a particular nation or region into IR theory, for a legitimately "scientific" theory should seek "universality, generality" (Song 2001; Choi 2008). Mainstream (positivist) IR theorists and methodologists argue that IR studies ought to seek observable general patterns of states' external behaviour, develop empirically verifiable "covering law" explanations, and test their hypotheses through cross-case comparisons. For example, Gary King, Robert Keohane, and Sidney Verba make it clear that generality is the single most important measure of progress in IR, stressing that "the question is less whether ... a theory is false or not ... than *how much of the world the theory can help us explain*" (King et al. 1994: 101, emphasis in original). From this perspective, any attempt to develop an indigenous IR theory, be it non-Western or Western, is suspect because it delimits the general applicability of theory. In the case of a Chinese IR theory, criticism of this kind can increasingly be found in studies by younger Chinese IR scholars. According to Xinning Song (2001: 68), Chinese scholars, especially younger ones who have studied in the West, think that it is "unscientific or unnecessary to emphasize the so-called Chinese characteristics."[2] A similar criticism can be found among Korean IR scholars in regard to attempts to build a "Korean-style" IR theory (Cho 2015). Those engaged in the "Korean School" of IR frequently ask: how can we make a distinctively Korean IR theory *while* trying to be as generalisable as possible? (see Choi 2008; Chun 2007; Min 2007; Min 2016). They agree that the Korean IR community needs to develop a theory that can explain the country's unique historical experience and geopolitical situation, but they also maintain that such a theory "will be judged by [the] strict measurements of scientific universalism" (Choi 2008: 209). In Jong Kun Choi's words (2008: 215), "Any theorizing based on Korea's unique historical experiences must be tested under the principle of generality."

Normative criticisms of attempts to build a "non-Western" IR theory highlight the relationship between power and knowledge. Critics point out that although theory-building enterprises from the perspective of the "non-West" commonly begin by problematising Western-dominated IR, the ongoing scholarly practices and discourses associated with "non-Western" IR can also entail (or reproduce) the same hierarchic and exclusionary structure of knowledge production, which can fall prey to particular national or regional interests. For example, in his discussion of Chinese visions of world order, William Callahan doubts the applicability of *Tianxia*. He claims that what the notion of *Tianxia* does is "blur" the conceptual and practical "boundaries between empire and globalism, nationalism, and cosmopolitanism"; rather than help us move toward a "post-hegemonic" world, *Tianxia* serves as a philosophical foundation upon which "China's hierarchical governance is updated for the twenty-first century" (Callahan 2008: 749). Supporting this view, Ching-Chang Chen (2011: 1) argues that

> re-envisioning IR in Asia is not about discovering or producing as many "indigenous" national schools of IR as possible. Scholars ... must also recognise and resist the pitfalls of equating the mere increase of non-Western voices with the genuine democratization of the field, if they are to live up to their responsibility to jointly construct a non-hegemonic discipline.

In a similar vein, Josuke Ikeda (2011: 12–13) argues that "there needs to be a 'post-Western' turn rather [than a] 'non-Western' [one] ... in order to address another kind of 'Westfailure' in IR theory." In short, critics argue that although it is our responsibility to make IR more pluralistic and democratic, "most intellectual endeavors to construct non-Western IRT in Asia run the risk of inviting nativism" (Chen 2011: 16).[3] Most recently, Andrew Hurrell (2016: 150) has added that although developing culturally specific ways of understanding the world "undoubtedly encourages greater pluralism," attempts to do so can also lead to "a cultural and regional inwardness that may work to reproduce the very ethnocentricities that are being challenged."

Response: "Global" IR

Sharing these concerns, more recent studies have begun to pay greater attention to the globalisation of IR in an attempt to transcend the West/non-West divide. Amitav Acharya is probably the most passionate scholar in this regard. In his presidential address at the annual convention of the International Studies Association (ISA) in 2014, Acharya explained what "Global IR" is or should be. His background assumption is this: "The discipline of International Relations does not reflect the voices, experiences, knowledge claims, and contributions of the vast majority of the societies and states in the world, and often marginalizes those outside the core countries of the West" (Acharya 2014: 647). Yet, instead of arguing for a counter (i.e. non-Western) approach, he presented the possibility of "Global IR" as an aspiration that "transcends the divide between the West and the Rest" while suggesting that IR should be "a truly inclusive" discipline that recognises its multiple and diverse foundations.

Obviously, Acharya is not alone in his views. According to Braspenning and Baele's study of contemporary developments in IR theory, one of the key features of IR's "third debate" is that it is problematising the "parochialism of American international political discourse" (Braspenning and Baele 2010: 5; see also Ashley 1984: 229). In particular, critical IR scholars argue that the field has developed in the United States "in isolation" from contributions made in other parts of the world. In this respect, Steve Smith has notes that the discipline should be opened up to include both theoretical and geographical diversity. More specifically, he notes that IR needs to become more inclusive of work from scholars from other countries. This would enable IR to become "a non-hegemonic discipline" (Smith 1987: 204). More recently, drawing upon postcolonial and feminist literature, Ann Tickner (2011: 611) argues that IR should move towards "a more international and pluralist discipline that is built on less West-centric foundations and is more respectful of multiple ways of understanding our complex world." In addition, "Global IR" is one of the key issues being addressed in the newly established Routledge book series *IR Theory and Practice in Asia*.[4]

What is missing in the debate? (Neglected) issues at stake in building "non-Western" IR theory

To summarise, an ongoing debate is based on the shared conviction that a pluralist approach to IR (be it "non-Western," "post-Western," or "Global" IR) is a good thing, and the terrain of this ongoing debate embraces a wide range of socio-epistemic concerns with varying emphases.

However, despite such a meaningful debate over "broadening" the theoretical and practical horizons of IR and its recent contributions, several critical questions and issues remain unclear and under-explored. For example, neither advocates nor critics properly address acute issues and contested implications associated with "non-Western" IR theory building, namely theoretical pluralism. Although calls for the "democratisation," "globalisation," and "diversity" of IR theory frequently appear in discussions, they remain a plea or an aspiration *without* specifying how they can be realised. Further, diversity in IR theory is often deemed to be an undisputed and appropriate premise upon which the attempts to search for national or regional "characteristics" are undertaken *without* pondering the manifold and contested implications that should actually be drawn from the premise.

The remainder of this chapter intends to identify what is missing in the debate. I suggest that there are (at least) three sets of questions that require more careful attention in our discussion of "non-Western" IR. First, does IR need to embrace pluralism? Second, to what extent has contemporary IR become pluralistic? Third, should IR pursue the promotion of dialogue and engagement across theoretical and spatial divides? Of course, each of these questions invites several subsequent questions. For instance, the question of whether pluralism needs to take place in IR requires us to think through the extent to which the field ought to embrace pluralism. Likewise, the normative "ought to" question related to dialogue and engagement leads to additional questions, such as that of "how to." I elaborate on these questions and their implications in the ensuing pages.

Does IR need to embrace pluralism? If so, how much?

Obviously, epistemic pluralism is a core premise upon which "non-Western," "post-Western," and "Global" IR projects are all founded. As discussed earlier, "non-Western" IR theory-building enterprises reject the long-lasting dominance of Western/American IR scholarship over the field and are dissatisfied with the corresponding marginalisation of non-Western worlds in international studies. Their advocates persistently argue for the "broadening" of IR beyond the disciplinary dominance of a particular region and call for embracing a wider range of theoretical, historical, or normative perspectives (see Acharya and Buzan 2010; Tickner 2011; Hutchings 2011; Ling 2013, 2014; Acharya 2014, 2016; Qin 2016). In Acharya's words, IR should "not impose any particular idea or approach on others but [respect] diversity," and it should be grounded in "world history, theoretical pluralism" (Acharya 2016: 4–5). Qin's "relational theory" of international relations, which emphasises "multiple cultures" and the high degree of "intimacy" in our "pluralistic world" (Qin 2016: 39), is an attempt to give theoretical substance to Acharya's idea of "pluralistic universalism."

Yet, a pluralistic approach as a "way of knowing" is not without its critics. For example, John Mearsheimer (2016: 147) has explicitly stated that he disagrees with the growing calls for broadening the horizons of IR beyond American dominance. Van der Ree (2014: 218) claims that in IR, "plurality is mostly understood as a serious problem which needs to be overcome." There are a considerable number of IR scholars who favour epistemic unity or theoretical synthesis over pluralism. According to Brian Schmidt:

too much pluralism leaves us with a divided discipline that not only fails to speak with one voice, but cannot even agree on what we should be studying, focusing on, or seeking to explain. Pluralism, in other words, masks the fact that we have an *incoherent* field.

(Schmidt 2008: 298, emphasis added)

Michael Brecher and Frank Harvey are deeply concerned with the lack of progress and knowledge accumulation in the field, arguing that alternative and critical perspectives in IR "encompass an array of research programs and findings that are not easily grouped into a common set of beliefs, theories or conclusions ... [and have] difficulty agreeing on what they have accomplished." (Brecher and Harvey 2002: 2). It is for these reasons that several scholars propose an epistemic synthesis, which has variously been referred to as a "paradigmatic" synthesis of research traditions in IR (Brecher and Harvey 2002); the "theoretical integration" of different levels of analysis (Hudson 2007); "analytic eclecticism" based on the mixing and matching of approaches (Sil and Katzenstein 2010; Cornut 2015); "multi-method" research that combines quantitative and qualitative methods and "middle-ground epistemologies" that combine positivist and interpretivist epistemologies (Collier and Elman 2008; Bennett 2015); and an "ontological" synthesis based on "quantum consciousness theory" (Wendt 2015).

However, this scepticism of pluralism is not representative of the majority of IR scholarship. Rather, many scholars, whether or not they are engaged in "non-Western" IR theorisation, tend to believe that IR should become more pluralistic (George 1989; Ashley and Walker 1990; Kratochwil 2003; Wight 2006; Braspenning and Baele 2010; Lebow 2011; Jackson 2011, 2015; Dunne et al. 2013a; Campbell 2013; Mearsheimer and Walt 2013; Ferguson 2015). Nonetheless, this does not justify the taken-for-granted acceptance of pluralism, which is strongly embedded across different forms of the "non-Western" IR theory-building enterprise. The point is that pluralism as such is not without controversy, although the view appears unproblematic among proponents of "non-Western" IR. Therefore, advocates for opening up IR ought to more fully address the epistemic implications of its underlying premise, namely diversity and pluralism.

What is more, although it is generally agreed that diversity and pluralism are "desirable" for a "better future" for IR (Kratochwil 2003; Hellmann 2003; Dunne et al. 2013b; Jackson 2015; Acharya 2016), we also have to address *how much* – in other words, to what extent – IR should embrace pluralism. This question is of great importance in the ongoing debate because the answer affects the degree to which the contour and the contents of the "non-Western" IR theory-building enterprise are to be either expanded (facilitated) or narrowed (constrained). Nevertheless, even in recent studies that make significant contributions to the study of "Global" IR, this question is either ignored entirely or treated as something that can be "put aside" (Bilgin 2016: 5). I think the question of whether and to what degree IR needs to embrace pluralism can only be answered *after* we have a clear understanding of the *current* state of diversity in IR. Put otherwise, we need to first examine and comprehend where IR currently stands in terms of diversity in order to determine where it should stand.

To what extent has IR actually become pluralistic?

Contemporary IR literature in general and arguments regarding "non-Western" IR theory in particular have a slim understanding of the extent to which contemporary IR has become diverse and pluralistic; this is mainly due to their partial and limited attention. The simplest way to understand the extent of diversity in IR scholarship is to look at how many knowledge claims exist. Even so, to understand diversity in this numerical sense is not as simple as it may appear, because knowledge claims are associated with several complex dimensions, including ontological, epistemological, theoretical, methodological, praxical, and geographical ones. Furthermore, even if we zoom in on one of these, the "theoretical" dimension, we need to look at diversity in terms of not only the number of theories available in the field, but also the epistemological, methodological, and empirical aspects of diversity, for all of them relate to theory building and theory testing.

Unfortunately, however, the ongoing debate tends to focus attention on only the theoretical dimension; furthermore, theoretical diversity tends to be approached narrowly, in terms of the *geographical origins* of key IR concepts, theories, or theorists. For example, Acharya's call for "Global IR" rests on the geopolitical assumptions that IR often "marginalizes those outside the core countries of the West" and that scholars beyond the Anglo-American core have the capabilities and resources necessary to render IR "truly" global (Acharya 2014: 647). This claim is made along geographical or geopolitical lines: either inside or outside of the West. In this sense, Wemheuer-Vogelaar et al. (2016: 18) argue that "geography plays a central role in the Global IR Debate," and that "the Global IR literature repeatedly categorizes scholars into … regional and national schools." Interestingly, Wemheuer-Vogelaar et al.'s study (2016: 24), based on the 2014 TRIP survey data,[5] shows that non-Western IR scholars "are more likely to have geographically bounded perceptions of IR communities" than their Western counterparts.

To be clear, this is not to say that it is not true that non-Western worlds are under-represented in international studies, or that this under-representation is unproblematic. The point is not that these geographically based concerns are misplaced, but that the current terrain of the "non-Western" or "Global" IR debate needs to extend to issues of epistemology and methodology in order to see the extent of the "parochialism" of IR more clearly and, thus, ameliorate it. This is especially necessary given that there are conflicting views of the extent to which IR has actually become diverse and pluralistic. A cursory survey of the IR literature on pluralism and the sociology of the field will suffice to illustrate this point.

On the one hand, some scholars argue that the discipline has *already* become pluralistic and diverse. For example, Nicholas Rengger notes that contemporary IR is "a plural, and pluralist, field. ... Whether one likes it or not ... that is simply the reality" (Rengger 2015: 32). Likewise, Tim Dunne, Lene Hansen, and Colin Wight argue that "IR now seems to have settled into an uneasy truce on the question of pluralism" due to "the proliferation of theories" in the discipline (Dunne et al. 2013a: 405, 416). On the other hand, the argument that IR is still monistic and parochial is also repeatedly made, not only in the "non-Western" or "Global" IR literature, but also in the IR literature on post-positivism and reflexivity. A recent work by Inanna Hamati-Ataya is a case in point. Calling for "strong reflexivity," she argues that "three decades after the launch of the post-positivist critique ... reflexive IR ... remains located at the margins of the margins of the discipline" (Hamati-Ataya 2013: 670; 2014: 171–172). Similarly, in a discussion of the state of theoretical diversity in IR, Christian Reus-Smit (2013: 604) observes that "[t]raditionally, mainstream International Relations scholars (and political scientists) confined the field to empirical-theoretic inquiry on [positivist] epistemological principle. ... The tenuous nature of this position is now widely acknowledged, increasingly by mainstream scholars." And David Lake argues that "positivists either subsumed the critiques offered by the reflectivists ... or just simply ignored and marginalized them" (Lake 2013: 570). It is in this respect that Patrick Jackson calls for "a broad and pluralistic definition of science" based on a variety of ontologies (Jackson 2011: 19). Given all of the above, the following question arises: what types of diversity are we talking about? Depending on our answer to this question, our understanding of the extent to which IR has become diverse and pluralistic will vary substantially, as will our rationales for and approaches to the "non-Western" and

"Global" IR projects. For example, if projects to broaden IR consider the issue of the hierarchy of knowledge in terms of not only geography (i.e. Western-centric IR theory), but also epistemology and methodology (i.e. the dominance of positivism), then their proposals can find common ground with post-positivist IR scholarship, whose epistemological underpinnings are marginalised by both the West and the non-West. I will develop this argument further in Chapter 2.

In short, the hierarchy of knowledge and scholarship is an issue that cuts across several realms of inquiry in IR, beyond the geopolitical influence or geohistorical origins of theory. In particular, the lack of diversity in IR can be seen in terms of epistemology and methodology, as my empirical investigation in Chapter 2 shows. For example, specific methodological injunctions that flow from positivist epistemology of science, such as operationalisation, quantification, empirical observation, and generalisation, prevail over the entire discipline of political science, including IR. I will discuss this point and its implications in more detail in later chapters. As it stands, however, the lack of epistemological, methodological, or praxical diversity and how it is connected with the "marginalisation" of non-Western voices in IR do not receive the attention they deserve. Too much attention is being paid to only one dimension of diversity, namely the geographical origins or historical foundations of theory.

***Should IR promote dialogue across theoretical and spatial divides?
If so, how?***

What has been discussed thus far ultimately asks us to consider the issue of theoretical fragmentation, a potential offshoot of our persistent pleas for diversity and pluralism, as a way to address "the current West-centrism of IR" (Buzan 2016: 156). That is, regardless of whether we achieve a consensus on the extent and types of diversity that we (ought to) pursue, the goal would remain the same from the perspective of the "broadening IR" project, be it "non-Western," "post-Western," or "Global" IR. To put it in the simplest terms, a shared goal means more diversity. This, however, can raise concerns about the fragmentation of IR scholarship. The more diverse IR becomes, the more divided and fragmented the discipline is likely to become, which is a hindrance to knowledge accumulation. This, as mentioned earlier, is part of the reason that some IR scholars take issue with pluralism (Schmidt 2008).

In response, scholars working on broadening IR, particularly in the name of "Global IR," often suggest that IR needs to engage in more active "dialogue" across theoretical and spatial divides. The scholars are not calling for discarding or disavowing Western-centric IR, but rather for rendering it broader and more inclusive so that voices and experiences outside the West are reflected more fully. Acharya (2014: 649) makes this point clear:

> My main argument is that while one cannot and should not seek to displace existing (or future) theories of IR that may substantially originate from Western ideas and experiences, it is possible, through dialogue and discovery, to build alternative theories … that have their origin in the South.

Furthermore, "encouraging debate and dialogue across perspectives … is a *core* purpose of the Global IR project" (Acharya 2016: 14, emphasis added).

Encouraging dialogue is not as simple as it may appear, however. As Kimberly Hutchings aptly notes, "dialogue" can be a mere exchange or encounter that is already "staged and scripted" by the mainstream (namely, in the case of IR, the West and positivists); as such, it could turn out to be "a piece of rhetorical bullying" (Hutchings 2011: 645). Furthermore, a "staged and scripted" dialogue across theories can lead to a tug of war between rival camps over truth claims and a turning inwards. For instance, David Lake (2013: 580) suggests that IR ought to pursue working "*within* paradigms" rather than working "*between* paradigms." In his words, "[t]he field would be better off … achieving progress within each approach according to its own criteria for success" (Lake 2013: 567).

Despite these concerns, many IR scholars, including Hutchings and Lake, do not oppose dialogue per se. Indeed, "vigorous" dialogue across cultures and regions and active engagement between theoretical perspectives are frequently proposed by those who wish to broaden IR. Moreover, this is also the case in reflexive discussions regarding the prospects of IR and IR theory. The "integrative pluralism" advanced by Dunne, Hansen, and Wight is a case in point. In "The End of International Relations Theory?" they argue that IR should move towards "integrative pluralism" in which not only diversity, but also, and more importantly, "engagement" across competing theoretical paradigms is encouraged (Dunne et al. 2013a: 416–417). In a related vein, Patrick Jackson foregrounds "engaged pluralism," which "brings unlike elements into dialogue with one another without fusing them into a specious synthesis" (Jackson 2011: 207). More than a decade ago, Yosef Lapid argued that if "pluralism … is the most feasible and deserving destination for the international relations theory enterprise in the foreseeable future, then dialogue must figure prominently on our agenda at the dawn of the twenty-first century" (Lapid 2003: 129). In short, the importance of dialogue per se is readily acknowledged in the IR literature.

The question then is how we can ensure proper dialogue and engagement across theoretical and spatial divides without subjugating marginalised perspectives or engaging in a narcissistic turf war. This question is important because the discipline is already marked by a positivist–post-positivist divide. It is also important from the perspective of the "non-Western" theory-building project because what this project aims to achieve could fragment the field even further. And finally, it is also important because those who make a plea for active dialogue and engagement do not generally elaborate on how we could embark on this project. To be sure, there are a few exceptions (Hutchings 2011; Bilgin 2016); in general, however, our call for dialogue is not well matched by a corresponding development of proposals on *how* we can realise it. What is lacking is an assessment of when each approach offers a better understanding of given issues; where our research interests overlap and thus complement each other; and, most importantly, how we can find and expand points of contact across theories and regions. This final set of questions – namely, should and how should IR promote dialogue across theoretical and spatial divides? – is inseparable from the first two sets of questions; in particular: to what extent IR has become pluralistic and what types of diversity we are talking about or pursuing?

What is to be done?

The questions examined in this chapter cut to the heart of the project to broaden IR. Without addressing them, any attempt to advance "non-Western" or "Global" IR is likely to remain inchoate. As noted, our understanding of where IR currently stands – and where it should stand – in terms of diversity determines whether the contour and the contents of various forms of "non-Western" IR theorisation should be expanded (facilitated) or narrowed (constrained). Further, if epistemic unity or synthesis rather than epistemic pluralism is seen as facilitating progress in IR, then attempts to broaden IR, be they "non-Western," "post-Western," or "Global," must be avoided. Relatedly, the types of diversity we are (or should be) pursuing will affect how we approach the "broadening IR" project. In this context, we must first clarify the extent to which contemporary IR has become pluralistic by looking at multiple dimensions of diversity. Furthermore, we need to empirically investigate the disciplinary *practices* associated with the IR publication system and IR pedagogy. In addition, since our constant calls for more diversity in IR could further complicate the issue of disciplinary divides and theoretical fragmentation, we must determine how we can engage in productive dialogue that does not entail subjugation by a particular community in the field, be it from the West or the non-West.

As the above analysis has shown, however, the issues examined in this chapter remain largely under-illuminated in the ongoing debate. Of course, achieving consensus on these questions seems to be a tall order. I also have no definitive answers to them. However, consensus can never be a necessary condition for any scholarly debate in the social sciences. Even hard scientists work toward consensus formation without an absolute consensual foundation upon which to base their research. Hutchings (2011: 639) comments, rightly in my view, that "discourse helps us to expand the parameters of our disciplinary imaginations and pave the way for a new era of discovery." If so, the current debate over "non-Western" IR should become richer and wider, considering the complex issues at stake regarding theoretical pluralism and fragmentation more fully. With this in mind, the remainder of this book examines what is missing in our debate regarding "non-Western" IR theory building. Chapter 2 undertakes a literature review and an empirical analysis of the extent to which the field has actually become diverse and pluralistic. This investigation, of course, needs to consider diversity beyond the current limited focus on the geographical origins of theory. Chapter 2 takes this task on and concludes that it is not nearly as diverse as we may believe it to be. Chapter 3 draws attention to the mechanisms and processes of knowledge production and transmission in IR. Through its empirical investigation of publishing and teaching practices in Asian IR communities, it shows that the dominance of the *West* in international studies is synonymous with the dominance of *positivism*, a particular view of science that originated in the modern West. Put simply, another name for "the West-centrism of IR" (Buzan 2016: 156) is positivism-centred IR. The chapter examines how this Western/positivist-centric IR is constructed, maintained, and reinforced, placing special emphasis on the ways in which IR is researched and taught. It unmasks the conservative roles played by the IR publication system and pedagogy in reproducing mainstream understandings and standard methodology.

The remaining chapters are devoted to what is probably the most acute issue associated with the "non-Western" IR theory-building enterprise; namely, theoretical fragmentation and dialogue. As noted, the more diverse IR becomes, the greater the number of dividing lines that are likely to emerge and the more fragmented the already divided field will become, which is a hindrance to knowledge accumulation and progress in IR. This is one of the main reasons for critiques of attempts to increase diversity and promote pluralism in the field. In this sense, the issue of fragmentation and dialogue comes to occupy the centre of attention in Chapters 4 and 5. In particular, extant studies lack necessary insights into the ways in which we may engage in active and meaningful dialogue in a fragmented discipline. Chapters 4 and 5 attempt to develop specific ways in which such a dialogue can be promoted, especially across two very apparent dividing lines in the field. Chapter 4 focuses on the enduring divide between positivism and post-positivism. Chapter 5 addresses the growing concern over the "West–non-West" divide and demonstrates how Western-centric IR theory and indigenous knowledge of Asia can be interweaved. All of these discussions aim to move the divided and fragmented field of IR one step closer to becoming a dialogic community.

Notes

1 This book follows the convention of using "IR" to denote the academic discipline of International Relations and "international relations" to refer to its substantive domain of study (i.e. the practice of global politics).

2 Yaqing Qin (2011: 252), however, sees it differently: "more and more scholars and PhD students [are] striving to explore the Chinese indigenous resources as inspiration for theoretical breakthroughs."

3 This position was soon the target of counterarguments. Shiro Sato, for example, criticises Chen by arguing that "the discourse of anti-non-Western IRT would not only strengthen the hegemonic status of Western IR, but also *discipline* Asian Studies" (Sato 2011: 4–5, emphasis added).

4 See www.routledge.com/IR-Theory-and-Practice-in-Asia/book-series/IRTPA (accessed 6 February, 2017).

5 The Teaching, Research, and International Policy (TRIP) project conducts a periodic survey of IR scholars regarding teaching and research practices. The survey results and relevant data from TRIP are available at https://trip.wm.edu/home/index.php/data/data-overview (accessed 27 July, 2016).

2 The extent of diversity in IR
Multiple dimensions

Contemporary IR literature in general and the ongoing debate on "non-Western" IR theory in particular have a skewed understanding of where IR currently stands in terms of diversity, mainly as a result of their limited understanding of what diversity consists of. The extent of diversity in the field can and should be examined according to various dimensions, including epistemological, theoretical, methodological, praxical, and geographical. As noted, however, the ongoing debate tends to focus on only one of these dimensions, namely, the theoretical; furthermore, theoretical diversity tends to be understood narrowly, in terms of only the geographical origins of key IR concepts, theories, or theorists. Many advocates of "non-Western" IR theory building and individuals working on "Global IR" begin their quest with geographical concerns, commonly stating that IR is "too Western-centric." What they problematise is that a particular region and its scholars, universities, and journals dominate the field (see, e.g., Bilgin 2010; Kristensen 2015; Tickner 2013; Acharya 2014, 2016). This is a geographically understood notion of "West-centrism."

However, this starting premise and understanding does not extend beyond geographical or historical concerns to the realms of epistemology and methodology. In other words, the extent of epistemological, methodological, or praxical diversity and how they can be connected with the issue of "marginalisation" do not receive the attention they deserve in the ongoing debate on "non-Western" IR. This is a serious limitation. The Western parochialism of international studies can and should be considered and addressed from epistemological and methodological perspectives as well as in geographical terms. For example, if we consider the problem of the hierarchy of knowledge not only from a geographical perspective (i.e. Western-centric theory), but also in terms of epistemology and methodology (i.e. positivism's dominance of the field), then the "non-Western" IR theorisation project can have far-reaching repercussions with support from post-positivist IR scholarship, whose epistemological underpinnings are marginalised irrespective of their geographical locations or origins, be they the non-West or the West. At the same time, although a large group of critical scholars express deep concerns about the marginalisation of post-positivist scholarship within IR (see, e.g., Joseph 2007; Jackson 2011; Hamati-Ataya 2013, 2014; Reus-Smit 2013; van der Ree 2013), these scholars are not concerned with the geographical composition of the field. In short, while both groups are concerned with "marginalisation" and thus call for a pluralistic and broad field of study, their sets of concerns remain disparate.

Given this, it is necessary to examine the extent of diversity in the field according to *multiple* dimensions. That is, we first ought to clarify the extent to which contemporary IR has become pluralistic by looking at multiple aspects of diversity in order to determine whether the reasons given for the need to theorise a "non-Western" IR are well grounded and how we could further galvanise the project. For instance, if the current parochialism of IR is not only geopolitical, but also epistemological and methodological, ongoing "non-Western" IR theory-building projects must refocus their attention, broadening the range of their own questions and undertakings. In this context, the following analysis begins with a discussion of the current status of epistemological, theoretical, and methodological diversity in contemporary IR. This analysis involves an empirical investigation of publishing and teaching practices in both Western and non-Western IR communities.

Multiple dimensions of diversity in IR[1]

Epistemology

It seems reasonable to start with the 1996 book *International Theory: Positivism and Beyond*, which examined 40 years of epistemological and theoretical debates in IR. According to the book's editors, Steve Smith, Ken Booth, and Marysia Zalewski,

> The main intellectual concern of the book, reflected in its subtitle, is to examine the state of international theory in the wake of a set of major attacks on its positivist traditions. Note that this subtitle does not claim that positivism is dead in international theory, only that there is now a much clearer notion of its alternatives.
>
> (Smith et al. 1996: xi)

Yet what seems more intriguing is the conclusion of this volume. It concludes that positivism continue to dominate IR and that pluralism had not yet been achieved in the field. More specifically, the book's introduction notes that "for the last forty years the academic discipline ... has been dominated by positivism" and that "the inter-paradigm debate" of the 1980s was not actually much of a debate, since all three paradigms – realism, liberalism, and Marxism/structuralism – were "working under positivist assumptions" (Smith et al. 1996: 11). Smith further argues that "the current 'debate' between neo-realism and neo-liberalism becomes much clearer when it is realised that both approaches are firmly positivist" (Smith 1996: 11). In effect, all of the contributors to the book agree that despite "the massive attacks on positivism in the social sciences in recent years" (Smith et al. 1996: xii), the various "neo" or "critical" or "social" approaches that had entered into the discipline since the early 1980s had failed to constitute a powerful and coherent alternative to positivism. In particular, Richard Little, who traced theoretical plurality and developments in liberal theory, concludes that the rise of pluralism was not accompanied by the demise of realism, whose theoretical underpinnings are firmly based on positivist conceptions of science (Little 1996: 83–84). In short, although the book opens on the critical note that many were dissatisfied with positivism as an epistemological foundation, it ends with the cautionary note that our discipline was not as diverse as we might have thought it was.

The question is whether this is still true two decades later. Unfortunately, the answer seems to be yes. Questions such as "to what extent do positivist assumptions and approaches continue to dominate the discipline?" are still being asked. As will be demonstrated below, despite the fact that the horizon of IR, in particular its theoretical terrain, has become wider as a result of the emergence of post-positivism in the late 1980s, positivism remains the dominant influence in terms of determining valid/scientific knowledge claims. Before demonstrating this observation, however, there is one terminological issue that needs to be addressed: what does positivism actually mean in IR?

Positivism, as a particular philosophy of science, is a contentious term; thus, the extent to which positivism influences contemporary IR remains a matter of debate. Nonetheless, positivism in the social sciences can generally be understood along the following lines: it is committed to a single scientific method that is centred on "empirical observations"; it believes in the necessary distinction between "facts" and values; and it aims to identify general patterns of observed phenomena (i.e. "facts") in order to develop empirically verifiable explanations and predictions (see Giddens 1974; Bryant 1985; Laudan 1996). In the context of IR, positivist studies attempt to determine observable general (or regular) patterns of states' external behaviours and develop empirically verifiable "covering law" explanations of international relations based on hypothesis testing and cross-case comparison (see, as a representative and influential work, King, Keohane, and Verba 1994). International relations studies is heavily dominated by positivist epistemological and particularly methodological concerns (for a similar observation, see Jackson 2015: 13–14). A large majority of scholarly works in IR tend to present an explanatory (as opposed to normative or constitutive) theory, derive testable hypotheses from that theory, and evaluate these hypotheses using (mainly) quantitative data. In short, although various post-positivist and "reflectivist" approaches have come to permeate the discipline in the last two decades, IR has not yet moved beyond positivism. Let me clarify this point by reviewing the pertinent literature on the positivist–post-positivist divide in more detail and examining publishing and teaching practices in IR communities.

First, Inanna Hamati-Ataya's observations are worth being quoted at length. She calls for "strong reflexivity" because post-positivism is "superior" to positivism (Hamati-Ataya 2014: 155, 171–172). In one of her articles addressing and promoting "reflexivism" in IR, Hamati-Ataya comments:

> The notion of "reflexivity" has been so intimately tied to the critique of positivism and empiricism in International Relations (IR) that the emergence of post-positivism has naturally produced the anticipation of a "reflexive turn" in IR theory.
>
> (Hamati-Ataya 2013: 669)

Nonetheless, she then admits the following:

> Three decades after the launch of the post-positivist critique, however, reflexive IR has failed to impose itself as either a clear or serious contender to mainstream [positivist] scholarship.
>
> (Hamati-Ataya 2013: 670)

This conclusion is also drawn by many scholars who have accepted post-positivism and related reflexive theorisation as valid forms of knowledge and have, thus, called for a more pluralistic, expansive form of IR both theoretically and philosophically. For instance, when discussing philosophy in IR, and particularly scientific realism, Jonathan Joseph complains that "the ontological implications of positivist assumptions can be seen in most aspects of realist, neorealist and other 'rationalist' theories of IR" (Joseph 2007: 349). Since Waltz's 1979 work, he argues, "we can see more clearly how mainstream IR is underpinned by positivist assumptions" about state behaviour; namely, assumptions about "rational behaviour, taking states as the (atomistic) units of analysis, employing a billiard-ball model of state interaction, focusing on regularities and predictable outcomes, and generally presenting a reified social ontology that excludes underlying structures, causal mechanisms or constitutive processes" (Joseph 2007: 349). Similarly, in a discussion of the state of theoretical diversity in IR, Christian Reus-Smit observes that "[t]raditionally, mainstream International Relations scholars (and political scientists) confined the field to empirical-theoretic inquiry on [positivist] epistemological principle. ... The tenuous nature of this position is now widely acknowledged, increasingly by mainstream scholars" (Reus-Smit 2013: 604). David Lake goes further, arguing that diverse approaches under the heading of reflexivism are likely to make the present debate in IR "less salient, as the assault on the positivists was less unified than in the past cases. [...] No approach won this debate, although the positivists remained ensconced at the centre of the field" (Lake 2013: 570–571). Then he delivers his verdict: "Positivists either subsumed the critiques offered by the reflectivists ... or just simply ignored and marginalised them" (Lake 2013: 570). In short, IR is seen as a field of study in which the dominance of positivism remains largely intact.

"Analytical eclecticism"

Some might take issue with the above characterisation of IR, reminding us of the "analytical eclecticism" of the discipline. They could argue that "pluralities of explanations" are both possible and being produced thanks to the "eclectic or problem-driven" approach, which advocates a "complexity-sensitive research agenda" (Cornut 2015: 50). If, as a number of researchers observe, IR now "inhabit[s] a theoretical terrain where ... 'analytical eclecticism' is the order of the day" (Wight 2013: 327) and "the majority of work in our field since its founding has likely fallen into the eclectic study" (Lake 2013: 572), could we not claim that IR is not in fact largely limited to positivist understandings and representations?

No. Surely, analytically eclectic research in IR prefers an inclusive, multicausal mode of inquiry to an exclusive, monocausal one; yet its conceptual baggage and thus immediate substantive analysis are narrowly confined to the three (American) mainstream theoretical perspectives of realism, liberalism, and constructivism. Additionally, based on the "factors" that eclecticist research selects and combines within the three theoretical perspectives, "analytical eclecticism" is firmly grounded in empiricism/positivism. For example, as Reus-Smit (2013: 599) rightly observes, the constructivist analysis incorporated into eclectic research practices in IR focuses on "social norms" in lieu of "society," as the former are believed to be "more readily characterized and analyzed as measurable dependent and independent variables." In other words, eclecticist research combines material capabilities (realism), economic interests and institutions (liberalism), and state identities or social norms (constructivism), all of which are relatively easily observable, quantifiable, and generalisable.

In positivism, the ability to observe, operationalise, and generalise factors, events, and processes is the most important criterion for the validity of "scientific" knowledge claims (see Van Fraassen 1980; Bryant 1985). It is thus important to remember that although the ever-growing analytical eclecticist discussion draws upon the insights of diverse theoretical paradigms, the epistemological foundation of the "mixing and matching" remains positivistic. Consider Sil and Katzenstein's following statements. While they note that analytical eclecticism intentionally – or, to use their term, "pragmatically" (Sil and Katzenstein 2010: 415–417) – "bypasses" epistemological or ontological issues in social science research, they also acknowledge that it is an "empirical" research programme. In their words, "the challenge may be greater when traveling across traditions, but it is not insurmountable if proper care is taken to consider the premises upon which specific analytic components are *operationalized* in relation to the *empirical* world" (Sil and Katzenstein 2010: 415, emphasis added). Put simply, analytical eclecticism is "an empirical-theoretic project" intended to address empirical problems and puzzles, and the theoretical insights of eclectic research are thus "*explanatory*[,] however diverse they might be" (Reus-Smit 2013: 591, emphasis added). Analytical eclecticism's (implicit or explicit) attention to and emphasis on "empirical terms" is the core reason that Reus-Smit complains about the analytical eclecticist position advocated by Sil and Katzenstein, instead calling for "a more ambitious form of analytical eclecticism" that "breaks established epistemological boundaries to bridge empirical and normative inquiry" (Reus-Smit 2013: 597–604). Jeffrey Checkel (2013) offers another, related criticism. In his recent work, which examines the state of theoretical pluralism in IR, he takes issue with the fact that analytical eclecticism disregards metatheory, epistemology, and macro-level critical ideas while focusing exclusively on problem-solving theories based on middle-range theorisation.

Methodology

Positivist principles and tendencies are especially clear in IR methodology. In effect, the specific methodological principles of positivism – such as operationalisation, quantification, empirical observation, and generalisation – prevail throughout political science.[2] The fact that quantitative methods and statistical methodology dominate the field of political science has significant implications for IR, which is dominated by political science (for a more detailed account of the methodological narrowness of US political science and the question of the disciplinarity of IR, see Jackson's forthcoming work, "'Does it Matter if it's a Discipline?' Bawled the Child"). Jackson notes that "the dominance of Political Science in international studies" may be "headquartered in the United States, but it is certainly not confined to the United States."

Many IR researchers, relying on the Humean conception of causation, tend to believe that the study of international relations ought to seek out observable general patterns in states' external behaviours. For example, Gary King, Robert Keohane, and Sidney Verba's *Designing Social Inquiry* – which "has strongly influenced the methods of study of many contemporary liberal, realist and even constructivist theorists in IR" (Kurki 2007: 361) – makes clear that generality is the single most important measure of progress in IR, stressing that "the question is less whether ... a theory is false or not ... than *how much of the world the theory can help us explain*" (King et al. 1994: 101, emphasis in original). As such, causal analysis in IR is often considered to be dependent on "quantitative regularity analysis" for identifying "general patterns" of "observed" events and processes, and it is held that causal-explanatory inferences follow from general cross-case demonstrations of a correlation. In short, many scholars, whether using deductive-nomological analysis or inductive-statistical methods, employ a positivist method for explanation; namely, the covering law model.

Perhaps this is what led David Lake to posit that while quantitative and qualitative research appear to be "two distinct cultures," they are actually "two variants of the same positivist approach. There is now substantial agreement on the basic methodology of and standards for positivist social-scientific research" (Lake 2013: 578, 579). As Colin Wight has aptly pointed out, all of this suggests that positivism dominates the discipline, "particularly in influential methods texts, such as ... KKV's [King, Keohane, and Verba's] volume" (Wight 2013: 328). Clearly, in the last three decades significant progress has been made in elaborating humanistic and interpretive methods that avoid commitment to outright positivism (see, e.g., Brady and Collier 2010; George and

Bennett 2005); yet there is little doubt that *mainstream* IR methodology is perceived as being grounded on a "scientific" positivist epistemology, while interpretive approaches are perceived as "unscientific." What is more, positivist methodology, which is centred on hypothesis testing with the ultimate aim of generating "nomothetic" generalisations, has become "virtually synonymous with 'good research' per se" in contemporary IR scholarship (Jackson 2015: 13–14; see also Mearsheimer and Walt 2013).

"The title of science"

Several scholars – including Monteiro and Ruby (2009), Kurki and Wight (2013), and Jackson (2011) – have raised an important issue regarding the so-called "science question" in IR: how is science defined in IR, and what does that imply for the study of international relations? Despite their different foci, these scholars all find that positivism continues to have a powerful and unyielding influence on the discipline. For instance, Nuno Monteiro and Keven Ruby's careful review of the long history of the "science" debate in IR clearly reveals the continued influence of (various forms of) positivism in IR's persistent attempts to legitimise itself as a scientific field of study. They suggest that we embrace an attitude of "foundational prudence" that is open-minded about philosophical foundations and thus "encourages theoretical and methodological pluralism" (Monteiro and Ruby 2009: 32). Their suggestion is, of course, based on the premise that positivism still dominates IR's understanding of what constitute valid/scientific knowledge claims; otherwise, their call for "foundational prudence" would make no sense.

Milja Kurki and Colin Wight make a similar observation in arguing that "[t]he influence of positivism as a philosophy of science has shaped not only how we theorize about the subject, and what counts as a valid question, but also what can count as valid forms of evidence and knowledge" (Kurki and Wight 2013: 15). More importantly, they rightly observe that "[s]uch is the influence of positivism on the disciplinary imagination that even those concerned to reject a scientific approach to IR tend to do so *on the basis of a general acceptance of the positivist model of science*" (Kurki and Wight 2013: 16, emphasis added). In a similar vein, Jackson comments: "In many ways, the field has not gotten beyond the situation that Wendt lamented in 1992, in which 'Science [positivism] disciplines Dissent [post-positivism] for not defining a conventional research program, and Dissent celebrates its liberation from Science'" (Jackson 2011: 182). As Roy Bhaskar said more than 30 years ago, positivism continues to usurp "the title of science" (Bhaskar 1978: 8).

Viewed in this light, "debate" seems an unfitting term, although it is often said that IR is currently organised around cleavages constituting the fourth (or third) "debate" – a debate between positivism and post-positivism, or between rationalism and reflexivism (Wæver 1996; Keohane 1988; Lapid 1989). Post-positivism neither fully engages in the "debate" nor plays the role of a clear counterpart. The bottom line is that for a large part of the intellectual history of IR, positivism has dominated and continues to dominate our conduct of inquiry in almost every realm, whether philosophical, methodological, or analytical, while post-positivism "has failed to translate into a clear, appealing alternative to positivism" (Hamati-Ataya 2013: 670).

The foregoing discussion implies that the IR world is a positivist one and that the "pluralist turn" is really a "plea" without a substantive set of practices. This is a particularly important point in that the existence of diverse theoretical approaches is one thing, but praxis is quite another. While the former might be a necessary condition for a pluralistic field of study, it is not a sufficient one: this diversity of theoretical approaches must be matched by corresponding practices in research and teaching.

To what extent is post-positivist research "practiced" in IR?

It has been more than three decades since post-positivism made its entry into the field. Since the third (or fourth) "great debate" in the 1980s – a debate between "rationalism" and "reflectivism" (Keohane 1988; Lapid 1989; Wæver 1996) – IR scholarship has begun to accept diverse post-positivist (or "reflectivist," to use Robert Keohane's term) approaches; namely, critical theory, feminist theory, constructivism, post-structuralism, and scientific realism. The overall theoretical terrain of contemporary IR has now become wider thanks to the emergence and development of post-positivism. An important question associated with this change is: to what extent is post-positivist research *practiced* in IR? As mentioned earlier, a large group of IR scholars continue to express deep concerns about the "marginalisation" of post-positivist scholarship within the field (see, e.g., Joseph 2007; Jackson 2011; Hamati-Ataya 2013, 2014; Reus-Smit 2013; van der Ree 2013), while others discuss the specific characteristics of pluralism (e.g. "disengaged," "engaged," and "integrative" forms of pluralism) with a conviction that IR is "a plural, and pluralist, field … [w]hether one likes it or not" (Rengger 2015: 32; see also Lebow 2011: 1220; Dunne et al. 2013b: 7). Neither group, however, offers the empirical evidence needed to sustain its arguments, which necessitates the investigation this chapter intends to undertake.

Here, I focus on the existing mainstream of IR (i.e. American IR) and on the newly emerging Asian (i.e. Chinese) IR community. The reasons for choosing these two particular IR communities are twofold. First, American IR has maintained a powerful disciplinary influence by force of its institutional and financial resources, as well as the hard power of the United States (Walt 2011). Furthermore, American IR continues to act as "the epicentre for a worldwide IR community engaged in a set of research programs and theoretical debates" (Ikenberry 2009: 203), and as J. Ann Tickner (2011: 609) aptly points out, American IR is legitimated by Europe (discussed below). As such, it is necessary to understand the status of post-positivist scholarship in the American IR community by examining its research and teaching practices in order to identify the influence of post-positivism in the field.

Second, several scholars have expected that "US parochialism" and "growing interest in IR outside the core [the United States], in particular, in 'rising' countries such as China" would lead to the rapid waning of American disciplinary power while opening up new spaces for the study of international relations (Wæver 2007; see also Tickner and Wæver 2009; Acharya and Buzan 2010; Arlene Tickner 2013: 629). Peter Kristensen and Ras Nielsen argue that "the innovation of a Chinese IR theory is a *natural* product of China's geopolitical rise, its growing political ambitions, and discontent with Western hegemony" (Kristensen and Nielsen 2013: 19, emphasis added). As such, an examination of the study of IR in China would generate important and interesting evidence that could help us discern the extent of theoretical diversity in IR.

In addition, it is well known that Chinese scholars have been trying to develop an IR theory with "Chinese characteristics." Yaqing Qin of China Foreign Affairs University asserts that it "is likely and even inevitable" that a Chinese IR theory will "emerge along with the great economic and social transformation that China has been experiencing" (Qin 2007: 313). In this regard, Marxism, Confucianism, "Tianxia" (天下, "all-under-heaven"), the Chinese tributary system (朝贡体制), and the philosophy of Mao Zedong and Deng Xiaoping are all brought in as theoretical resources of "Chinese IR" (see, e.g., Song 2001; Qin 2007, 2011; Kang 2010; Y.-k. Wang 2011, 2013; Xuetong 2011; Wan 2012; Horesh 2013). Although consensus on what these "Chinese characteristics" actually are is yet to be achieved, Marxism is always presented as one of them. As Xinning Song of Renmin University of China comments, it is frequently argued that "Chinese characteristics should consist of fundamental tenets of Marxism" (Song 2001: 68).

For these reasons – first, the anticipation that existing American disciplinary influence in IR will decrease due to China's rise and, second, attempts within China to develop an alternative IR theory with "Chinese characteristics" – Chinese IR scholarship has been selected as a case in order to determine the extent to which post-positivist research, including that of critical theory, has come to permeate this newly emerging scholarly community.

In addition, there is no single study, let alone a comparative analysis, of the present status of post-positivist IR scholarship in China that focuses on both publishing and the teaching practices of the Chinese IR community. Assuredly, there are quite a number of studies on "Chinese IR" (see, e.g., Song 2001; Callahan 2001; Qin 2007, 2011; Shambaugh 2011; Wan 2012). However, (the extent of) the practice of post-positivist research is not the primary concern of these studies; instead, they offer either a general overview of how IR as a discipline has evolved in China or an analysis of whether an indigenous IR theory should be developed in China. Furthermore, even in recent studies on the extent to which "Chinese IR theory" has advanced (Qin 2007, 2011; Wan 2012), the focus is limited to the examination of the publications of Chinese IR scholars without looking into IR teaching in China.

Research and teaching practices in American IR

Since there are a number of excellent studies that explore how IR is researched, published, and taught in the United States, the following investigation builds on this work. Let us first consider the comprehensive research of Daniel Maliniak and his colleagues, which analyses recent trends in IR scholarship and pedagogy in the United States using two sets of data – every article published in the field's 12 leading journals (of which 8 are published in the United States) from 1980 to 2007[3] and the results of three recent surveys of IR faculties at four-year colleges and universities in the United States.[4] Their findings show that there is a strong and increasing commitment to positivist research among American IR scholars. More specifically, they found that about 58 per cent of all articles published in the 12 major journals in 1980 were positivist, and that this had increased to almost 90 per cent by 2006.[5] As well, around 70 per cent of all American IR scholars surveyed described their work as positivist. More importantly, younger IR scholars were more likely to call themselves positivists: "Sixty-five percent of scholars who received their Ph.D.s before 1980 described themselves as positivists, while 71% of those who received their degrees in 2000 or later were positivists" (Maliniak et al. 2011: 454; for details see pp. 453–456). In this context, Maliniak et al. note that there is "a remarkable and growing consensus within the US academy that a positivist epistemology should guide IR research." (Maliniak et al. 2011: 454) It should therefore come as no surprise that "since 2002 more articles published in the major journals employ quantitative methods than any other approach" (Maliniak et al. 2011: 439).

At the same time, the American IR community appears to enjoy "theoretical" diversity in the sense that no single theoretical paradigm dominates the community. It is a "limited" form of diversity, however, based on a clear commitment to positivism. According to the data provided by Maliniak et al.'s study, more than 70 per cent of the contemporary IR literature produced in the United States falls within the three major theoretical paradigms – realism, liberalism, and conventional constructivism – all of which lie within the "epistemological" ambit of positivism. Of course, constructivists are less likely to adopt positivism's traditional epistemology and methodology than scholars working within the other two theoretical paradigms; yet "most of the leading constructivists in the United States, unlike their European counterparts, identify themselves as positivist" (Maliniak et al. 2011: 454, footnote 42).

The fact that IR is largely organised around the three major theoretical paradigms is also clear in the classrooms of American colleges and universities. A series of surveys conducted by the Teaching, Research, and International Policy (TRIP) Project[6] shows that IR faculty in the United States devote a great deal of time in introductory IR courses to the study or application of the major theoretical paradigms, particularly realism, the theoretical underpinnings of which are based on positivism. While its share of class time may have declined, realism still dominates IR teaching in the United States. For example, 24 per cent of class time in 2004, 25 per cent in 2006, and 23 per cent in 2008 were devoted to this paradigm; these percentages are larger than for any other theoretical paradigm. The data also shows that the IR faculty members surveyed in the United States spent none of their class time on one of the representative post-positivist perspectives, namely, feminism, in 2004; the amount of class time devoted to it had increased by 2008, but it still remained low, at 5 per cent. Much the same can be said about non-traditional and more critical IR approaches, including critical theory, critical war studies, postcolonialism, and post-structuralism (see the TRIP report, Maliniak, Peterson, and Tierney 2012: 12–15). Obviously, this is not to suggest that IR teaching in America is solely dedicated to the three mainstream paradigms with a sole commitment to positivism, only that class time does not properly reflect the wide range of IR theories and diverse post-positivist perspectives.

Not surprisingly, this trend is consistent with the content of American IR textbooks. Elizabeth Matthews and Rhonda Callaway's content analysis of 18 undergraduate IR textbooks currently used in the United States demonstrates that most of the theoretical coverage is devoted to realism, followed by liberalism, with constructivism a distant third (Matthews and Callaway 2015). For example, realism appears on more than 28 per cent of the pages, and liberalism on more than 21 per cent, of one of the major IR textbooks, Henry R. Nau's (2015) *Perspectives on International Relations: Power, Institutions, and Ideas*. In addition, on average, realism and liberalism appear on 15 per cent of the pages of the all textbooks analysed, which is a higher percentage than that reached by any other theoretical paradigm. Likewise, realism and liberalism have the highest number of tables and figures, while other theories, such as feminism, lag far behind (for more details, see Matthews and Callaway 2015: 197–199).

These findings indicate that the bulk of IR studies and teaching practices in the United States is committed to epistemological and methodological positivism. Many pertinent studies concur with this observation (see Lipson et al. 2007; Mead 2010; Hagmann and Biersteker 2014; Kristensen 2015). Given the enduring and powerful influence of the American scholarly community on the configuration of the field of IR, this worries those who support post-positivist research and a pluralist IR.

Research and teaching practices in Chinese IR

One aspect that could be more worrying from the perspective of post-positivist or pluralist IR scholars is the lack of difference between mainstream and Chinese IR. The latter also lacks sufficient attention to alternative or critical approaches.

An investigation of all articles published by China's four leading political science and IR journals – 现代国际关系 (*Journal of Contemporary International Relations*, JCIR), 世界经济与政治 (*Journal of World Economics and Politics*, JWEP), 国际政治研究 (*Journal of International Studies*, JIS), and 外交评论 (*Journal of Foreign Affairs Review*, JFAR) – over 20 years (1994–2014) shows that virtually no studies used post-positivist theory. My research team first searched the databases of China's National Social Science Database (CNSSD, http://www.nssd.org/) and China's National Knowledge Infrastructure (CNKI, http://epub.cnki.net/KNS/) – both of which provide full-text Chinese scholarly articles published in more than 9,900 journals across the social sciences – in order to identify major journals in which Chinese articles on international relations, international political economy, international security, and foreign policy are published. With the findings, we undertook a further investigation of the publication databases of all academic political science and IR organisations based in China, including the China National Association for International Studies.

In addition, in an effort to ensure the representative nature of the journals to be examined, we also identified the journals in which studies by political science and IR faculty members at the top 15 Chinese universities, including Beijing University, Fudan University, Renmin University of China, and Tsinghua University,[7] appeared most frequently by analysing their research CVs as well as the journal publication data gathered from the CNSSD and the CNKI. This data was once again cross-checked with the results of our earlier investigation of the publications and publication outlets of Chinese political science and IR organisations. We found that JCIR, JWEP, JIS, and JFAR are leading academic journals in the field of IR in China, with 11,607 articles published in Chinese in these journals during the 20-year period from 1994 to 2014.

Subsequently, an in-depth keyword-based search – in both Chinese and English,[8] using both online materials (i.e. HTML or PDF versions) and printed issues – of all of the articles was carried out in order to determine how many of them used post-positivist approaches. The keywords used fit into six broad sets of categories: post-positivism, critical theory, feminist theory, scientific realism, post-structuralism, and constructivism. In each category, more specific terms and the names of scholars relevant to the representative categories were coded. For example, the keyword category of "critical theory" included eight related terms in both Chinese and English: critical international relations, critical security studies, critical sociology, Frankfurt School, Jürgen Habermas, Robert Cox, Richard Ashley, and emancipation.

In the category of "constructivism," we included "Alexander Wendt," as well as "Friedrich Kratochwil" and "Nicholas Onuf," even though Wendt's constructivism walks a fine line between positivism and post-positivism, lying well outside positivism's traditional ambit from an ontological perspective while largely subscribing to its epistemological tenets (Wendt 1995, 1999; for a similar observation, see Rivas 2010).[9] A different research strategy was adopted in the case of feminism. The centrepiece of my investigation is *post*-positivism, and feminist IR theory can be either positivist or post-positivist. Given this, I chose (among other keywords) "J. Ann Tickner" and "Christine Sylvester" as search terms as they are representative scholars working on post-positivist feminist theory.

In total, six sets of keywords and 38 related terms were used in our survey. The results show that Chinese IR has little interest in post-positivist research; of the 11,607 articles analysed, only 569 studies (4.9 per cent) relate to post-positivism. This figure includes articles that merely mention any of the 38 related terms (see Table 2.1). Furthermore, recall that the figure includes articles that discuss Alexander Wendt and his constructivism, which borders on positivism. Given all of this, the number of articles directly committed to post-positivist research is likely to be much smaller than 4.9 per cent. For example, when the name "Alexander Wendt" is excluded, the figure drops to 4.2 per cent.

In effect, our survey indicates that most theoretical IR studies in China use one of two major theoretical paradigms – neorealism or neo-liberalism – both of which lie within the methodological and epistemological ambit of positivism. More specifically, we first carried out a series of keyword-based searches with the following 11 general terms: realism, neorealism, balance of power, power transition, hegemony stability, liberalism, neo-liberalism, institutionalism, transaction cost, democratic peace, and economic interdependence. The findings were then cross-checked with a close reading of all abstracts of the articles surveyed. The results show that 78 per cent of the theoretical articles surveyed fit within the two major theoretical paradigms; interestingly, most of the articles focus on neo-liberalism.

Recent studies on developments in IR theory in China reach similar conclusions (Qin 2011; Chen 2011; Wang and Blyth 2013). For instance, David Shambaugh, who has undertaken keyword searches of article titles and abstracts published between 2005 and 2009 in Chinese IR-related journals, concludes that realism, liberalism, and constructivism dominate Chinese IR theory articles – with realist articles being the most numerous (Shambaugh 2011: 347). Similarly, Yaqing Qin (2011: 249) acknowledges that "most of the research works in China in the last 30 years have been using the three mainstream American IR theories [realism, liberalism, and constructivism]" – with liberalism having an edge – although Chinese scholars have made considerable attempts to establish a new IR theory that reflects "Chinese characteristics." Again, recall that Marxism is widely considered one of the key "Chinese characteristics." Menghao Hu even writes: "There are many different kinds of IR theories in the world. But in the final analysis there are only two. One is Marxist IR theory and the other is the bourgeois IR theory" (Hu 1991, quoted in Song 2001: 64). Further, Marxism, in various forms, underlies critical theory's normative analysis and understanding of what theory should do (Devetak 2014: 420–421). Nevertheless, as the survey has confirmed, critical theory, one of the representative theoretical approaches of post-positivism, remains at

Table 2.1 Post-positivist research in Chinese IR

Keywords and related terms (searched in Chinese and English, using both online materials and printed issues)						
Sets of keywords	后实证主义 (Post-positivism)	女性主义/女权主义 (Feminism)	批判理论 (Critical theory)	科学的实在論/科学实在论 (Scientific realism)	建成主义 (Constructivism)	后结构主义 (Post-structuralism)
Related terms	后实证学派 (Post-positivists) 反思主义 (Reflectivism) 反思性 (Reflexivity) 解释学 (Hermeneutics) 解释主义 (Interpretivism)	女性主义者 (Feminist) 社会性别 (Gender) 女权主义立场论 (Feminist Standpoint) 主从关系 (master-slave relationship) 辛西娅·安罗 (Cynthia Enloe) 克瑞斯汀·丝维斯特 (Christine Sylvester) 安·蒂克纳 (Ann Tickner)	批判的国际关系 (Critical international relations) 批判的安保学 (Critical security studies) 批判社会学 (Critical Sociology) 法兰克福学派 (Frankfurt School) 罗伯特·考克斯 (Robert Cox) 艾逊礼 (Richard Ashley) 西蒙弗洛伊德 (Jürgen Habermas) 解放解开 (Emancipation)	实在论** (Realism) 实在主义者 (Realist) 超越/超迈的实在论 (Transcendental Realism) 批判实在论 (Critical Realism) 罗伊·巴斯卡 (Roy Bhaskar) 罗姆·哈瑞 (Rom Harré)	社会的建构 (Social Construction) 社会理论 (Social theory) 国际政治社会理论 (Social theory of international politics) 国际规范 (International norm) 亚历山大·温特 (Alexander Wendt) 尼古拉斯·奥努夫 (Nicholas Onuf) 约翰·鲁杰 (John Ruggie) 克拉托克维尔 (Friedrich Kratochwil)	后现代主义/後現代主義 (Post-modernism) 后现代性 (Post-modernity) 康培尔 (David Campbell) 雅克·德里达 (Jacques Derrida) 米歇尔·福柯 (Michel Foucault)

Number of the keywords and related terms and names found in major Chinese journals

JCIR	22	43	9	1	40	25
JWEP	117	41	12	9	135	24
JIS	29	10	17	5	31	6
JFAR	47	4	12	3	29	14
Total	125/12,465 * (1.0%)	98/12,465 (0.8%)	50/12,465 (0.4%)	18/12,465 (0.1%)	234/12,465 (1.8%)	69/12,465 (0.6%)

Sources: 中国国际关系学会, www.cnais.org; 外交评论, http://wjxy.chinajournal.net.cn; 中国现代国际关系研究院, www.cicir.ac.cn/chinese; 现代国际关系, www.cicir.ac.cn/chinese/bookView.aspx?cid=136; 台灣政治學會, www.tpsahome.org.tw; China's National Social Science Database, www.nssd.org/; China's National Knowledge Infrastructure, http://epub.cnki.net/KNS/ (accessed 19 August, 2013 to December 20, 2016).

Notes: * Total number of articles published in the four major Chinese journals from 1994 to December 2015. ** The terms "实在论" (Realism) and "实在主义者" (Realist) coded above do not refer to political realism in the field of IR, which should be translated into "现实主义".

"the margins of the margins" of the Chinese IR community, being addressed in only 0.3 per cent of studies. It is, to use Shambaugh's term, a "negligible" theory in China.

This is an interesting but disappointing finding, particularly for those engaged in moving IR beyond the long-standing American disciplinary dominance and toward a pluralistic field that embraces post-positivism and "Global IR" (Acharya 2014: 647). Assuredly, there are also a few China-based journals that publish articles in English rather than Chinese; these include *Journal of Chinese Political Science* and *Chinese Journal of International Politics* (CJIP). In particular, CJIP is worthy of further inspection here, for this journal, which was recently listed in the Social Science Citation Index, is currently managed by the Institute of Modern International Relations, Tsinghua University, and publishes articles in English with the aim of advancing not only "the systematic and rigorous study of international relations," but also "Chinese IR" based on the so-called "Tsinghua Approach" (Zhang 2012: 73).[10]

Yet a search of all articles published in CJIP from 2006, when the journal's first issue came out, until December 2014 confirms that post-positivist research is on the margins of the Chinese IR community; a total of 131 articles were published in CJIP during that period; among them, only 12 mention or discuss post-positivism.[11] What is more interesting is that the seven most-cited sources in CJIP are *not* Chinese journals, but major "American" journals, such as *International Security, Journal of Conflict Resolution, International Organization, World Politics*, and *International Studies Quarterly* (see Table 2.2).[12]

As demonstrated above, there is little epistemological or theoretical diversity in those US-based journals. As an example, recall Maliniak et al.'s

Table 2.2 The seven most-cited sources in *Chinese Journal of International Politics*

Title	Editorship and/or managing institutions
International Security	Belfer Center for Science and International Affairs, Harvard University, USA
Foreign Affairs	Council on Foreign Relations, USA
Journal of Conflict Resolution	University of Maryland, USA
International Organization	University of Wisconsin-Madison, USA
World Politics	Princeton University, USA
International Studies Quarterly	International Studies Association
American Political Science Review	American Political Science Association, USA

comprehensive study, which shows that almost 90 per cent of all articles published in these journals since 2006 are positivist (Maliniak et al. 2011: 455). In short, there is little difference between research trends in American IR and those within the newly emerging Chinese IR scholarship in terms of the prevailing influence of positivism.

This trend in the Chinese IR community is also discernible in *teaching practices*. An examination of the curricula of all political science and IR departments at the top 15 universities in China shows that there is no single graduate seminar or undergraduate IR course designed to teach post-positivism-related theories, including feminist theory and critical theory. In addition, I analysed the syllabi of the major Chinese universities' introductory IR theory courses for the 2013–2014 academic year; this investigation of Chinese IR courses and teaching practices is based on 23 syllabi gathered from 21 faculty members who teach and/or conduct research in international politics at major Chinese universities. The findings of the investigation indicate that realism, liberalism – particularly neoliberal institutionalism – and "conventional" constructivism account for the vast majority of class time, whereas almost none of the major theories or concepts of post-positivism appear in the syllabi.

Of course, Chinese universities do offer (a limited number of) IR classes that teach post-positivist theories along with their positivist counterparts. Yet, as the survey has shown, these are exceptions. Furthermore, when post-positivism is discussed in the IR classroom in China, almost all of the core readings are devoted to constructivism, particularly constructivism-related books and articles written by leading *American* constructivists, who often identify as positivists. In sum, the investigation of the teachings of Chinese IR reinforces the earlier finding that post-positivist research remains at the margins of IR, especially in terms of practice.

European IR – scholarship that "did grant American IR a 'scientific' legitimacy"

Compared with the American and Chinese IR communities, European IR is often thought to embrace a more pluralistic approach to the study of international relations, and thus there seems to be a more diverse range of IR scholarship in Europe. The English School of IR theory and its historical analysis are a representative example. Ole Wæver (1998: 711) notes that the British IR community is "uniquely diverse." Interpretivism, along with (or as opposed to) positivism, is also preferred in other parts of Europe, including France, Germany, and the Netherlands, when it comes to "doing IR" (see Hellmann 2014). Consider, for example, the Copenhagen School of security studies and its preference for interpretivist approaches. Despite this diversity in European IR theory and methodology, one should recall that it is indeed "American IR" that commands a dominant presence in the institutional structure of the discipline. As G. John Ikenberry (2009: 203) comments, American IR, "as a modernist social science," is still "the epicentre for a worldwide IR community engaged in a set of research programs and theoretical debates." More importantly, the current American institutional preponderance in IR is not solely a matter of geographical location and the nationality of scholars. Assuredly, the educational, national, and ethnic backgrounds of scholars working in the United States are diverse, probably more so than in any other country. This preponderance is also a matter of the specific and unyielding commitment to positivist epistemology and methodology by scholars working in the United States, especially in terms of defining how to undertake the study of international relations.

Conclusion

Contrary to the general expectation, research and teaching trends in the American and Chinese (and Asian) IR communities are quite similar in terms of epistemology and methodology. This is not because Chinese (and Asian) scholars are trying to emulate their American counterparts, however, but because they believe that a positivist approach to "doing IR" – an approach that remains mainstream in the United States – is "normal" and "scientific." Irrespective of Chinese IR's intentions to develop an indigenous theory, this trend contributes to consolidation of the hegemonic status of positivist international studies and the institutional preponderance of American IR. For example, even Yan Xuetong, a Chinese scholar who advocates the development of "Chinese IR" theory as an alternative to Western- (American-)centric IR, emphasises the importance of "scientific methods," which he defines in empiricist terms. In an interview with Creutzfeldt, he further notes that the use of "the scientific method" makes it "easy ... to communicate with each other" (Creutzfeldt 2012): this point will be addressed in detail in the next chapter.

Put simply, although the present "geographical" composition of IR might indicate that we are increasingly moving toward "internationaliza-tion" (Turton 2016), the predominance of a US-centred discipline and US-led commitments to positivist methodologies remains unabated. As a result, diversity, particularly epistemological and methodological diversity, is still lacking in the global structure of IR. The above empirical examination and literature review confirm the dominance of positivism in the field while showing that post-positivist research has failed to become a powerful contender. Furthermore, as will be discussed in more detail in the following chapter, a strong commitment to positivism is also visible not only in mainstream (i.e. American) IR and the rapidly emerging Chinese IR community, but also in other Asian IR communities. For example, Japan and South Korea demonstrate clear tendencies to embrace positivist understandings of and approaches to science, and to use Western-centric methods and concepts exclusively.

Once again, IR research and teaching is more diverse in Europe than in the United States or Asia. As a result, a wider range of post-positivist IR theories appear be recognised in Europe. Nonetheless, there is still a need to understand the common commitment to positivism among the American and Asian IR communities in order to make sense of the current and prospective status of pluralism in the discipline. More importantly, as J. Ann Tickner (2011: 609) points out, Europe "did grant American IR a 'scientific' legitimacy." As briefly discussed earlier (and as will be discussed in detail later), this so-called "science question" in IR has great ramifications for constituting, shaping, changing, or maintaining the theoretical and methodological terrain of the discipline. And the long history of the "science" debate in IR clearly indicates the continued influence of (various forms of) positivism in the persistent attempts to legitimise IR as a scientific field of study (Monteiro and Ruby 2009: 32). Kurki and Wight (2013: 15) further comment that the influence of positivism on the conduct of inquiry in IR is so great that even those who wish to reject a scientific approach to the study of international relations tend to do so *on the basis of a general acceptance of the positivist model of science.*

In sum, it seems clear that we continue to live in an intellectual "monoculture" (McNamara 2009) marked by the hegemony of positivism in empirical-praxical, conceptual, and methodological terms, which has significant implications for the various forms of the "non-Western" IR theory-building enterprise. The current parochialism of IR, which concerns all those engaged in "non-Western" IR theorisation, is not only geographical. As the above analysis demonstrates, Western/ American dominance in the field can also be seen in the dominance of positivism. A crucial question, then, is why IR scholarship (in both the American/Western and non-Western/Asian IR communities) is so strongly committed to positivism. In order to achieve "a truly inclusive and universal discipline" (Acharya 2016: 4–5) that embraces a wider range of experiences, knowledge claims, and theoretical perspectives, the ongoing "broadening IR" projects – be they "non-Western," "post-Western," or "Global" IR – ought to understand how positivism continues to dominate the field across regions. In brief, why is IR a positivist/Western-centric discipline?

Notes

1 The discussions in the following sections draw and expand upon my previous work (Eun 2016).
2 For a general review of methodological pluralism in contemporary political science research and curricula, see Yanow and Schwartz-Shea's 2010 "Perestroika Ten Years After: Reflections on Methodological Diversity" and Mead's 2010 "Scholasticism in Political Science," both of which conclude that the discipline has not gone far enough in terms of diversity. Their studies show that qualitative methods and interpretive research are currently marginalised in the discipline, suggesting that the "Perestroika" movement for promoting a more pluralist methodology is still needed.
3 These journals are *International Organization, International Security, International Studies Quarterly, Journal of Conflict Resolution, Security Studies, World Politics, Journal of Peace Research, Journal of Politics, American Political Science Review, American Journal of Political Science, British Journal of Political Science*, and *European Journal of International Relations.*
4 Maliniak et al. (2011) identified 4,126 individuals who were researching and/or teaching IR; 1,719 scholars responded to their surveys.
5 Maliniak et al. (2011: 455) code "positivist" works as those "that implicitly or explicitly assume that theoretical or empirical propositions are testable, make causal claims, seek to explain and predict phenomena."
6 Since 2004, TRIP has surveyed faculty members at colleges and universities who teach or conduct research on international relations in more than 20 countries, including the United States, Canada, and the United Kingdom. The surveyed countries do not include China. For further details, see https://trip.wm.edu/home/.
7 The others are Nanjing University, Zhejiang University, Shanghai Jiao Tong University, University of Science and Technology of China, Wuhan University of Technology, Sun Yat-Sen University, Tianjin University, Wuhan University, East China Normal University, Harbin Institute of Technology, and Dalian University of Technology. These universities were selected according to the "Times Higher Education Asia University Rankings 2014," which analyses 13 performance indicators to provide comprehensive and balanced comparisons. See www.timeshighereducation.co.uk/world-university-rankings/2013-14/regional-ranking/region/asia/ (accessed 11 June, 2015).
8 In addition, we employed both Mandarin and Cantonese in our Chinese keyword-based search.
9 See, for example, the following statement by Wendt: "the epistemological issue is whether we can have objective knowledge of these [socially constructed] structures" (Wendt 1995: 75).
10 See www.oxfordjournals.org/our_journals/cjip/about.html (accessed March 11, 2015).

11 The investigation is based on the data gathered from the CJIP website (http://cjip.oxfordjournals.org/ accessed 7 May, 2015). The texts and abstracts are accessible on the website. As before, a keyword-based search was undertaken, using the 38 post-positivism-related terms.

12 This is consistent with what Peter M. Kristensen found in his study of the geography of IR, which concludes that US-based journals and institutions continue to dominate IR (see Kristensen 2015: 249–257).

3 Why is IR so Western/positivist-centric?

As the examination of diversity in several realms in IR – in particular the empirical investigation of publishing and teaching practices in Asian IR communities – in Chapter 2 has demonstrated, the dominance of the West in international studies is synonymous with the dominance of positivism, a particular perspective on and approach to science derived from the West and premised on the modern Western philosophical understanding of rationality. Put simply, another name for "the West-centrism of IR" (Buzan 2016: 156) is positivism-centred IR. There is thus a need to understand the mechanisms and processes through which "Western/positivist-centric" IR is constructed, maintained, and reinforced. In particular, it is necessary to have a clear understanding of how positivist epistemology and methodology dominate global IR communities, including those of Asia, given the ultimate objective of "non-Western" IR theory building; namely, more diversity in IR theory and greater pluralism in the discipline. That is, in order to rectify the current parochialism of IR, advocates of "non-Western" IR first need to understand why they too are living in the same narrow world dominated by positivism.

Why has IR failed move beyond positivism despite our persistent calls for a pluralistic IR and "a considerable, in fact quite an over-whelming, literature" on post-positivist scholarship (Kurki 2015: 780)? This failure is all the more puzzling considering that it has been more than three decades since various post-positivist theories entered into IR as "massive attacks" on positivism (Smith et al. 1996: xi). Further confusion arises from the fact that there have long been welcoming statements on diversity and pluralism in the discipline. In attempting to answer this question, I first review the pertinent litera-ture in order to identify the "shared answers" given to IR questions. Then I offer some complementary thoughts from a socio-epistemic perspective.

Literature review: Searching for "shared answers"

Let me begin to address the question of why IR has failed to move beyond positivism by considering a common-sense response. Positivism, as a way of producing truth claims, is fully satisfying, so there is no need to go beyond it. Of course, we know – at a common-sense level – that this answer is inadequate. *Post*-positivism began with a rejection of and dissatisfaction with positivist epistemological and methodological assumptions and their dominance in IR. Furthermore, in the philosophy of science – from which IR scholarship has imported several theories and concepts in order to ground the discipline on "an unshakable 'scientific' foundation" – the positivist orthodoxy "began to crumble" in the 1970s; its hegemonic position has now been overthrown (Wight 2002: 40; see also Hollis and Smith 1990: 67; Monteiro and Ruby 2009: 15). This makes the questions raised at the outset of this chapter more puzzling. If positivism is no longer a "secure" foundation in the philosophy of science, why is positivism still the prevailing stance within IR, a discipline that frequently turns to the philosophy of science in search of "scientific" credentials?

Limitations of post-positivism

A more plausible answer than the common-sense response is that there is a clear need for an alternative to positivism, but post-positivism has failed to assert itself as a clear contender. Three reasons for post-positivism's failure are commonly given. First, post-positivist scholarship is terminologically and conceptually ambiguous; second, there is no shared epistemological platform on which "distinctly different" post-positivist theories can stand together; and third, post-positivists reject a positivist approach to science without proposing an alternative (see, e.g., Smith 1996: 32; Brecher and Harvey 2002; Guzzini 2013; Jackson 2011; Kurki and Wight 2013; Lake 2013; Hamati-Ataya 2014). Let me discuss these points in turn.

It is often claimed that terminological and conceptual ambiguity hinders the growth of post-positivist IR scholarship. For example, consider the reflexive observation of Hamati-Ataya, who has been calling for "strong reflexivity" in IR on the grounds that post-positivist research is "superior" to positivism (Hamati-Ataya 2014: 155, 171–172). She explains that although "'reflexivity' has indeed gained a substantive visibility in IR debates and literature," a quick review of the literature is likely to reveal

> a substantially large range of variations on the terms "(self-)reflection" and "(self-)reflexion." An obscure combination of these may even be found in one single text, … [which] refer[s] to "reflexivity,"

"self-reflexivity," and "self-reflection" all at once, without explaining the differences among these terms.

(Hamati-Ataya 2013: 670, 673–674)

Put simply, despite its frequent use in post-positivist scholarship, "reflexivity" is an elusive term; this in turn causes confusion with respect to what a post-positivist ontology is supposed to look like and what distinguishes the epistemological concerns of "reflexive" scholarship from those of other academic traditions in IR.

In his appraisal of the inter-paradigm debate, Steve Smith notes that

> the vast majority of international relations research over the last 30 years has rested implicitly on positivist assumptions. [...] All too often positivism-as-epistemology continues to play the same role as before. [...] [Meanwhile,] post-positivist accounts are working with distinctively different epistemologies; it is this which explains why there is no prospect of them constituting an alternative.
>
> (Smith 1996: 32, 34, 35)

Similarly, Michael Brecher and Frank Harvey, concerned by the lack of progress and knowledge accumulation in IR, argue that alternative and critical perspectives "encompass an array of research programs and findings that are not easily grouped into a common set of beliefs, theories or conclusions." They ask: "If those who share common interests and perspectives have difficulty agreeing on what they have accomplished to date, ... how can they establish clear targets to facilitate creative dialogue across these diverse perspectives and subfields?" (Brecher and Harvey 2002: 2). In other words, post-positivism conflates and confuses very distinct epistemological stances and philosophical concepts. Criticisms in this regard posit that although alternatives to positivism are commonly grouped together under the heading of post-positivism, in many respects, the only thing they have in common is a rejection of positivism (Kurki and Wight, 2013: 23).

Related to this point is the third reason: post-positivists either hesitate or resist specifying what constitutes good "science" and what scientific research into international relations should entail. "Even those concerned to reject a scientific approach to IR tend to do so on the basis of a general acceptance of the positivist model of science" (Kurki and Wight, 2013: 16). This implies that post-positivism either rejects the application of "scientific" methods to social phenomena (i.e. anti-naturalism) or challenges the notion and project of "science" altogether (i.e. anti-scientism) despite the fact that the philosophy of science embraces a wide variety of legitimate understandings of science (Archer et al. 1998; Hollis 2002; Patomäki 2002). Viewed in this sense, an important question that needs to be considered is "what exactly this non-positivist social 'science' is all about" (Guzzini and Leander 2006: 80).

All three of these reasons are relevant, with varying degrees of significance, to the question of why IR has failed to move beyond positivism. Several researchers have already begun to address these issues. For example, there have been recent attempts to cast new light on the function and purpose of science in IR and to refine (or broaden) conventional conceptions of science and causation (Kurki 2007, 2008; Jackson 2011; Suganami 2013). Stefano Guzzini, for example, has recently proposed four modes of theorising – "normative, meta-theoretical, ontological/ constitutive, and empirical" – each of which has a different yet "connected" scientific purpose (Guzzini 2013: 533, 535). Attempts have also been made to conceptualise reflexivity more rigorously and redress post-positivists' "mistaken conflation" of science (in general) with a particular version of science; namely, a positivist representation (Guzzini 2005; Lynch 2008; Joseph 2007; Joseph and Wight 2010; Rivas 2010, Hamati-Ataya 2013, 2014).

Disconnection between words and deeds?

We need to take a step back here and consider a more fundamental question: are researchers and students of international relations so familiar with the alternatives to positivism – namely, post-positivism and reflexivity – that we can confidently move on to deal with their major shortcomings in the hope of creating a more pluralistic field of study? If the aforementioned issues are adequately addressed, will a significant post-positivist alternative to positivism emerge? This is an important and fundamental question because prior to trying to overcoming the limitations of alternatives, one needs to be fully aware of what the alternatives actually are. Then we ought to ask ourselves whether or not our research and teaching practices have been rich enough to embrace the diverse approaches of post-positivism and encourage pluralism in the field. Unfortunately, however, none of us can claim with confidence that we have done enough in terms of research and teaching. Even when we advocate pluralism, we rarely practice what we preach, especially in the classroom.

A strong commitment to positivism by Asian IR communities

As demonstrated in Chapter 2, Chinese IR also employs a narrow range of theoretical, epistemological, and methodological approaches, even though Chinese scholars have attempted to develop a "non-Western" IR "with Chinese characteristics." For instance, an examination of 11,607 IR-related journal articles published in China over 20 years (1994–2014) clearly shows a shortage of studies on post-positivism in the Chinese IR community. Indeed, the results indicate that most theoretical IR studies in China are devoted to the two major theoretical paradigms of realism and liberalism, both of which lie within the epistemological and methodological ambit of positivism. Furthermore, the seven most-cited sources in *Chinese Journal of International Politics*, a journal advocating "Chinese IR" theory building, are not Chinese journals, but major "American" positivist journals (Maliniak et al. 2011: 455). In addition, an examination of the curricula of all political science and IR departments of the top 15 universities in China indicates that there is not even one graduate seminar or undergraduate IR course designed to teach post-positivism-related theories. When post-positivism is discussed in the IR classroom in China, almost all of the core readings are devoted to constructivism, particularly to the books and articles on constructivism written by leading American constructivists, who often identify as positivists. In short, most IR studies and courses in China are committed to positivism, while post-positivist research remains at the margins of the field.

Interestingly, and unfortunately from a pluralist perspective, a strong commitment to positivism is also visible in other Asian IR communities. For example, there have been numerous calls for an "indigenous" IR theory that can better explain local international politics in the South Korean IR community. However, as Young Chul Cho (2015: 682) observes, "American dependency" and "Western-centrism" continue to dominate the "Korean-style" IR theory-building enterprise. In other words, although it is often argued that Korea should develop a distinctively Korean IR theory (i.e. a "Korean School" of IR) on the basis of Korea's unique history or traditions, most Korean scholars explore how to develop a Korean IR theory and how to judge its success largely from a positivist perspective, considering American IR *the* global or central reference point. Jong Kun Choi (2008: 215), for instance, writes that "although Korean IR should strive to explain the country's unique historical experience, it will be judged by strict measurements of scientific universalism." In this regard, Cho (2015: 689) notes: "Korean scholars' increasing calls to build a 'Korean-style' IR theory is still operating under a colonial mentality, sustained by the hegemony of US IR's positivist metatheory, [which] might turn South Korea into a mere test bed of US IR's so-called 'scientific' models."

Japan, too, has a clear tendency to adhere to positivist under-standings of science and utilise mainstream (i.e. Western) methods and concepts of IR as the sole reference point in IR theorisation. Although some argue that Japanese contributions to IR, particularly those of pre-Second World War Japanese thinkers, should be considered original and receive greater recognition (Inoguchi 2007; Ikeda 2008), Japanese IR – as Ching-Chang Chen (2012: 463) shows in his analysis of recent developments in IR theory in Japan – "reproduces, rather than challenges, a normative hierarchy" embedded in Western-centric IR theories "between the creators of Westphalian norms and those [at] the receiving end." Similarly, Chen (2012: 478) argues that IR studies in Japan and South Korea have "much in common at the metaphysical level" because they both pursue "science" in a positivist manner and rely on mainstream Western (American) concepts to theorise interna-tional relations. Kazuya Yamamoto makes a similar observation about Japanese IR scholarship when he explores how international studies have evolved in Japan in the post-war period. While Japan continues to consider the idea of "pacifism" and taking a historical approach as central to the study of international relations and foreign policy, there has been growing interest in statistical and mathematical modelling in the Japanese IR community, as "scientific approaches to the social sciences … [and] research designs that seek generality and causality … have increasingly become popular" in political science fields in Japan (Yamamoto 2011: 274). In short, there is little difference between research trends in the American and Asian (Chinese, Korean, and Japanese) IR communities in terms of their commitment to positivist epistemology and methodology. This results in the predominance of positivism-centred teaching.

Do we practice what we preach?

Obviously, IR does involve diverse post-positivist theories. However, as mentioned, that diverse theoretical approaches *exist* does not necessarily mean that they are *practiced*. While the former might be a necessary condition for a pluralistic field of study, it is not a sufficient one. The investigation of publishing and teaching practices in IR communities in Chapter 2 shows that we do not practice what we preach. It seems that several IR scholars continue to express their deep concerns about the marginalisation of post-positivist scholarship in the field, regard-less of geographic location. For example, consider Hamati-Ataya's observation in the discussion of post-positivism and its key concept, reflexivity:

> While a review of the literature points to the significance the notion of reflexivity has acquired in contemporary IR, it also reveals the "reflexive turn" has failed to translate into a clear, appealing alternative to positivism, and therefore remains located at the margins of the margins of the discipline.
>
> (Hamati-Ataya 2013: 670)

This diagnosis is shared by many other scholars who accept post-positivism as a valid approach to knowledge production (see, e.g., Joseph 2007: 348–350; Jackson 2011: 207–212; Reus-Smit 2013: 604; van der Ree 2013: 30). More specifically, when Jonathan Joseph discusses the philosophy of science in IR with a focus on scientific realism, he complains that "the ontological implications of positivist assumptions" are clearly detected "in most aspects of realist, neorealist and other 'rationalist' theories of IR," whereas its alternatives (e.g. scientific realism) have not always received the attention they deserve in the study of world politics (Joseph 2007: 348, 350). Similarly, in the discussion of the state of theoretical diversity and the role of metatheory in IR, Christian Reus-Smit (2013: 604) writes that "[t]raditionally, mainstream International Relations scholars (and political scientists) confined the field to empirical-theoretic inquiry on [positivist] epistemological principle. ... The tenuous nature of this position is now widely acknowledged by mainstream scholars." Patrick Jackson also concurs with this point. In his 2011 book, *The Conduct of Inquiry in International Relations*, Jackson argues that different research paradigms, including the "reflexivist" paradigm, should be considered equally valid (or "scientific") modes of knowledge in IR, although they are not: in practice, "neopositivist" research is considered the most valid paradigm and "reflexivist" the least (Jackson 2011: 207–212).

All of this suggests that we, as researchers and teachers of IR, have not done enough to actualise a pluralistic IR. That is, our research and teaching in both the existing and emerging mainstreams of IR have fallen far short of including diverse approaches of post-positivism. The answer to the question posed at the beginning of this chapter – why has IR has failed to move beyond positivism? – is becoming clearer. Despite the support for pluralism in IR, researchers and particularly students are not adequately aware of alternative and critical IR approaches, the plausibility of their alternative accounts of science, or their usefulness, because we do not practice what we preach. We want to move beyond positivism toward pluralism, but we rarely act on this desire. The existence of various post-positivist theories in IR has not translated into disciplinary practice. Instead, a narrow range of positivist theories, concepts, and methods has dominated IR publishing and teaching. Because there is no substantive, systemic set of publishing and teaching *practices* for post-positivism or pluralism, students of IR are ill-informed of the strengths and limitations of alternatives to positivism. This in turn leads to reproducing (or reinforcing) the present (narrow) state of the discipline.

Looked at in this way, it is not only the three sets of shortcomings of post-positivism discussed at the beginning of this chapter – its terminological and conceptual ambiguity; its lack of a common epistemology; and the mistaken conflation of science (in general) with a particular version of science (positivism) – that is preventing the spread of pluralism, but also the field's limited knowledge and practice of post-positivism. Certainly, this is not to say that becoming more aware of the existence of various post-positivist perspectives guarantees pluralism, only that without recognising and practicing alternative but equally valid approaches to producing knowledge, we simply cannot move on to the next stage of solving the problems inherent in those alternatives.

Considering this, the real question seems to be how we can render IR more fully attentive to the fact that many legitimate (or potentially promising) ways of making knowledge claims exist "out there" – beyond positivism. This question appears simple, but answering it is not, because doing so requires answering why alternatives to positivism have not received the attention they deserve in both publishing and teaching. In sum, we need to go beyond tautologically arguing that we have to pay more attention to alternatives.

Socio-epistemic issues in pluralism

Once again, let us ask: will an active post-positivist scholarship serving as a powerful alternative to positivism emerge in contemporary IR if the limitations of post-positivism are adequately addressed? Here, it is worth mentioning that positivism, too, has serious limitations. Ontologically, it leads to a truncated and impoverished view of the rich and complex texture of world reality; epistemologically, it imposes unnecessary restrictions on the range of possible causes of social phenomena; methodologically, it suffers from theory-laden observation. In positivism, epistemology and ontology are tied together: what is known is what can be observed, and what "is" is what can be known – a view that Roy Bhaskar (1978: 28) has called an "epistemic fallacy." Put simply, many *actual* events never become *empirical*. For these reasons, among others, positivism has lost the prominence it once held in the philosophy of science (Wight 2002: 40). Furthermore, a voluminous literature criticises positivism from diverse perspectives across disciplines, including economics, where positivist principles have a firm grip on the conduct of research (see, e.g., Samuels 1980, 1990; Caldwell 2003).

Nonetheless, as seen earlier, most of the publications and teaching in American and Asian IR communities are replete with positivist stances and empiricist approaches. Whatever shortcomings alternatives to positivism may have, they are not the only reason that those alternatives are "located at the margins of the margins" of IR. In other words, regardless of their limitations, alternative lines of explanation and critical approaches should be taught at universities and appear in academic journals far more widely and frequently than has been the case thus far. This is especially so given that we have been calling for a more pluralistic IR and that it has been more than three decades since post-positivism was first considered in IR. Viewed in this light, the above question needs to be rephrased as follows: why does positivist research remain at the centre of IR despite its serious limitations?

Disciplinary socialisation and politics in IR

In his 1962 book, *The Structure of Scientific Revolutions*, Kuhn criticises the conventional view that science progresses by the accumulation of objective observations and empirical tests. Instead, he demonstrates that science has evolved through what he called "normal science"; namely, the process of hypothesis testing and "puzzle-solving" dictated by the existing major paradigm in a given scientific field. In a related vein, Kuhn's work on the history of planetary astronomy shows how scholarly communities working within the logic of "normal science" respond to anomalies that defy their core theoretical propositions. In simplified terms, mainstream theorists, wedded to the standard interpretations and methods that allow them to dominate their field, first tend to deny the anomaly and then to deem it trivial or transient. Then, as the salience of the anomaly becomes undeniable, scholars – especially younger scholars, less professionally invested in the standard approach – develop new or alternative theoretical lenses to explain the anomaly. If this new theoretical approach supersedes the old one, it becomes the new paradigm of inquiry even though the major proponents and practitioners of the existing paradigm rarely convert, even when they are confronted with overwhelming evidence that the new paradigm can explain more phenomena (or explain existing phenomena better).

This summary does not do full justice to Kuhn's argument, but it is sufficient for our purposes. Kuhn's most important argument is that "scientific," and thus acceptable, knowledge is in effect the sociological (by-)product of communal practices determined (or at least governed) by the major paradigm within a given scholarly community (Kuhn 1962; see also Kuhn 1970).

Kuhn's argument regarding the evolution of science has two important implications for IR. First, although they could drive a paradigm change, alterative and critical approaches in IR are currently trapped in the stage of being ignored or denied. Second, they are trapped not because mainstream positivist IR theories or epistemologies are without fault or their alternatives are worthless, but because "doing IR" based on positivist principles is seen as "normal." Positivist ideas and accounts have dominated IR throughout its history. Further, from the first great debate until the inter-paradigm debate of the 1980s, it has been positivists who have either dominated or won the debates in the discipline, which has allowed their approach to serve as the dominant paradigm. Once established as standard or common sense, the approach became so powerful that irrespective of whether it had serious weaknesses and was confronted with anomalies, it defined our analytical and practical horizons. That is, positivism, as the standard way of conducting inquiry in IR, determines what counts as the "valid" subject matter of IR and what counts as "acceptable" knowledge of international relations in both publications and teaching. Most IR scholars thus set their research problems on the basis of positivist epistemology and assess evidence produced by methodological procedures that correspond to the standard. In other words, all aspects of inquiry – the selection and framing of research questions, the representation and interpretation of relevant empirical observations, and the specification of evidentiary standards – are undertaken in accordance with the standard approach, which is naturally reflected in teaching.

This also applies to Asian IR communities. As discussed above, Japanese IR has recently seen "the rise of scientific [positivist] approaches to the social sciences"; relatedly, "research designs that seek generality and causality have increasingly become popular in political science fields in Japan" (Yamamoto 2011: 274). Much the same can be said about Chinese IR. For example, when the meaning (or purpose) of theory is taught or discussed in an IR classroom in China, what is largely invoked is a positivist understanding of the role of theory, namely, "generality" or "universality." Even in the discussion on building an IR theory with "Chinese characteristics," several Chinese IR scholars argue that such a theory – whatever "characteristics" or purposes it might have – "should seek universality, generality" in order to be recognised as a "scientific" enterprise (Song 2001: 68). Interestingly (and naturally, from a socio-epistemic perspective), this positivism-oriented understanding of theory and methodology is more easily discernible in studies by the younger generations of Chinese IR scholars who have attended American universities (Shambaugh 2011); these young Chinese scholars tend to remain sceptical of attempts to build an indigenous IR theory (Wan 2012). As the number of foreign-trained Chinese scholars returning to their homeland increases, we can expect that "the Gramscian hegemonic status of Western [positivist] IR" (Chen 2011: 16) will remain intact in China as a result of the various forms of social interaction between scholars at the domestic and international levels.

The emphasis on universality and generalisability can also be found among South Korean IR scholars concerned with "Korean-style" theory building. How can we make a distinctively Korean IR theory while trying to be as generalisable as possible? This is a key question in attempts to establish a "Korean School" of IR. For instance, Choi (2008: 209, 215, emphasis added) writes: "any theorizing based on Korea's unique historical experiences must be tested under the principle of generality. [...] Although Korean IR should strive to explain the country's unique historical experience, it will be *judged* by strict measurements of *scientific universalism*." This line of thinking is commonly found in the Korean IR community (see, e.g., Chun 2007; Min 2007). In this regard, Young Chul Cho (2015: 688) claims that South Korean social sciences are very much in line with American social sciences in the sense that both are "based largely on rationalist/positivist episte-mology." South Korean IR scholarship, he further notes, has "appeared to be a staunch disciple of mainstream IR. The whole of academia – particularly, political science and IR – in South Korea still tends to prefer American doctoral degrees to domestic or non-American ones." In this respect, it is widely acknowledged that "PhDs from the US have an advantage in the South Korean academic job market" (Cho 2015: 682; for other studies presenting similar observations, see Hong 2008; Park 2005; Yu and Park 2008). This situation can be seen as an offshoot of disciplinary politics and socialisation.

"Socialised" mechanisms through which the existing paradigm is reproduced

All of the above adds up to the consequence that "doing IR" based on positivist principles is considered normal. Just as states are socialised into the international system, IR scholars are socialised into the existing IR disciplinary system. This academic disciplinary socialisation entails selection, which tends toward the elimination of approaches or explanations that do not fit into the socialised – or, to put it more clearly, standardised – practice. In particular, the selection is reinforced by journal publication systems, and ideas or methods peculiar to the field's standardised approach tend to comprise the first cull. Moreover, socialisation within an academic discipline applies not only to scholars already working in it, but also, and more directly, to those who want to enter it. As Thomas Biersteker comments, "PhD candidates are educated in the canon of the discipline in order to enable them to engage in the core debates, as well as to be *marketable* in the broader discipline of political science" (Biersteker 2009: 318, emphasis added; see 310–318). This socialisation process causes graduate students to be oriented to the professional norms of their academic disciplines. Trapped between the pursuit of knowledge and the pursuit of a career, their motivations to work on new and/or critical approaches are sidelined. Jonas Hagmann and Thomas Biersteker (2014: 293) note that "IR schools worldwide instruct great numbers of students to adopt particular modes of thinking and approaches concerning world politics." The result is a sameness that makes for intellectual reproduction rather than theory development.

The result is that most of the articles published in major journals are positivist, and that statistical analysis, hypothesis testing, and data manipulation have become indispensable requirements in all IR methodology courses, with relatively little work and virtually no core courses dedicated to post-positivism. Given the nature of academic socialisation and politics, which entail reproduction of the standard understanding and approach, the answers to the following questions start to become clear: why is there a lack of praxis of alternatives to positivist epistemology and methodology within IR, and why is there a lack of diversity in IR publishing and teaching despite the serious limitations of positivism and the constant calls for pluralism?

Taken as a whole, it seems necessary to discuss the *practice* of pluralism in light of academic disciplinary socialisation, because what is at stake in developing a pluralistic IR is also what is at stake in current disciplinary socialisation practices. The existing paradigm is reproduced and reinforced by the ways in which IR is researched, published, and taught. Hence, if we can change these mechanisms to more fully recognise the validity of a wide range of epistemological, theoretical, methodological, and spatial perspectives, it may be possible to move IR toward becoming a pluralistic and inclusive discipline.

But how can these "socialised" mechanisms be changed? Because these mechanisms are "socialised," they tend to be stable and insusceptible to change. In Chapter 6, I suggest "reflexive solidarity," an encounter between self-reflexivity and collective solidarity. First, however, we have one more issue that should be addressed: the issue of fragmentation and dialogue. As discussed in Chapter 1, the existing IR literature lacks much-needed insights into *how* we can realise active and meaningful dialogue in IR, although it frequently calls for a dialogic vision of knowledge production. The same is true of the ongoing discussion regarding the "non-Western" IR theory-building enterprise. It is often said that "encouraging debate and dialogue across perspectives ... is a *core* purpose of the Global IR project" (Acharya 2016: 14, emphasis added); yet the question of how one might or should pursue this aim in this divided and fragmented field remains unanswered. The following chapters are devoted to developing specific ways of promoting such a dialogue. More specifically, Chapter 4 attempts to bridge the enduring divide between positivism and post-positivism, suggesting a shift in the points of contention from metatheory to method. Chapter 5 addresses the growing concerns about "the West–non-West" divide, showing how Western-centric IR theory and indigenous knowledge of Asia can be interweaved. Both chapters aim to move IR one step closer to becoming a dialogic community.

4 Broadening IR through dialogue
Bridging the positivist–post-positivist divide

That IR should pursue dialogue and engagement across theoretical divides, particularly the existing positivist–post-positivist divide, is largely uncontroversial. Many IR scholars argue that the goal should be to encourage not only diversity but also active engagement and dialogue across competing theoretical paradigms, and particularly between positivist and post-positivist paradigms (see Brecher and Harvey 2002; Smith 2003; Hellmann 2003; Lebow 2011; Tickner 2011; Hutchings 2011; Jackson 2011; Dunne et al. 2013a; Wight 2013). Different though the arguments are, they have a great deal in common. They all maintain that the overall theoretical terrain of contemporary IR has become richer and broader as a result of the emergence and development of post-positivism; namely, critical theory, feminist theory, (critical) constructivism, post-structuralism, and scientific/Critical Realism. At the same time, they all hold that the field will become fragmented and divided unless there is dialogue and engagement across these perspectives. This fragmentation impedes progress in our understanding of the "complexities" of today's world (Little and Smith 2006: 93–96). Furthermore, "pluralism *without engagement*" might lead to a nihilist perspective of epistemic relativism in which no one really bothers to adjudicate competing theoretical claims, with "each seeking to produce warranted assertions in their own way" (Jackson 2015: 13, 15; see also Dunne et al. 2013a: 415–416). This is pernicious to knowledge "accumulation," in particular the progressive accumulation of "theoretical" knowledge, and thereby to progress in IR (Brecher and Harvey 2002: 2).

The present state of IR appears to confirm these concerns. Although contemporary IR has a wider theoretical lens and more analytical tools than it previously did, the discipline is currently fragmented and dominated by monologue (Dunne et al. 2013a: 418; Lake 2013: 580). Barry Buzan and Richard Little (2001) note that IR has a particularly strong "tradition" of both inward-looking thought and fragmentation between research schools. They see this as one of the reasons "why International Relations has failed as an intellectual project." Gerard van der Ree (2013: 43) concurs, adding that in such a context of fragmentation and inter-school rivalry, the status of knowledge is often determined not by the validity of truth claims but by the "representational schemes" within which those claims are presented. Others also remain deeply concerned about the combination of inter-school rivalry and lack of dialogue, regarding the present state of affairs as one of the greatest obstacles to both enhancing our theoretical understandings and addressing complex and interconnected real-world issues. For example, Katzenstein and Okawara (2001/2002: 154) argue that intellectual discourse in IR has become increasingly dominated by "paradigmatic clashes in which champions extol the virtues of a particular analytical perspective to the exclusion of others" (see also Sil and Katzenstein 2010, 2011)They then conclude that this attitude "hinders efforts to understand the complexities of the world." Similarly, David Lake (2013: 571) argues that contemporary IR scholars, "positivist and reflectivist alike, have simply retreated to their own corners of a multi-sided boxing ring, occasionally tossing a punch in one or the other direction but more often talking amongst themselves and complaining of not being taken seriously by others." As he has also said, "[i]ntellectual progress does not come from proclaiming ever more loudly the superiority of one's approach to audiences who have stopped listening" (Lake 2011: 476).

A gap in the ongoing discussion on engagement and dialogue

It is in this respect that a considerable number of prominent IR scholars, including Lapid (2003), Sil and Katzenstein (2010), Jackson (2011, 2015), Hutchings (2011), Tickner (2011), and Dunne et al. (2013a), have all claimed that IR needs more dialogue and engagement. As Hutchings (2011: 640) aptly writes, "predominant strands of thought, both mainstream and critical, in the IR academy have traditionally welcomed dialogic exchange as part of the process of discovery of new truths." Nonetheless, these calls for dialogue tend to take the form of a plea, and they lack insight into how to achieve the desired goal (see, e.g., Jackson 2011: 188, 207–212; Dunne et al. 2013a: 407, 416; Wight 2013: 343–344). For example, Dunne, Hansen, and Wight argue that IR should move toward "integrative pluralism," in which not only diversity but also, and more importantly, "engagement" across competing theoretical paradigms is encouraged. But they do not discuss how to achieve this engagement in a divided IR. Without a fuller exposition of either *how* to encourage engagement or of *where* research concerns and interests overlap, they argue that the "ultimate test of integrative pluralism will be researchers from multiple perspectives engaging in the practice of pluralism through engagement with alternative positions where their concerns and research interests overlap" (Dunne et al. 2013a: 417).

In short, although those concerned about theoretical divisions and fragmentation in IR persistently call for engagement and dialogue, they do not elaborate how one might or should achieve this. If IR is to become a field of study involving active engagement and dialogue across theoretical paradigms, then we must go beyond the tautological advice to pay more attention or listen more carefully to each other. This is of enormous significance to IR, for the field remains pluralistic *and* "divided" (Lake 2013: 579), and it is likely to become more so as a result of "theoretical proliferation" (Dunne et al. 2013a: 408; Reus-Smit 2013) and the increasing interest in "non-Western" IR theory building. In what follows, I provide suggestions for some ways to engage in more substantive dialogue within the field.

How to encourage engagement and dialogue in a divided IR

Some careful thinking is needed at the outset. First, saying that we need to promote engagement and dialogue in a divided IR does not imply that we ought to aim for a "unified" field of study. The main purpose in calling for more engagement and dialogue is to help us deepen our understanding of complex international relations, not to unify knowledge in a particular realm of inquiry by recourse to a certain method. For example, when an engaged form of pluralism is discussed in the IR literature, what is referred to is mostly encouraging greater interaction and dialogue across theoretical paradigms while accepting the validity of a wide range of theoretical and methodological perspectives. This is hardly a call for epistemic unity. Even when Tim Dunne and his colleagues argue for "integrative" pluralism, they emphasise "more diversity than 'unity through pluralism' and more interaction than 'disengaged pluralism'" (Dunne et al. 2013a: 407).[1] Similarly, when Laura Sjoberg and J. Samuel Barkin propose "multiple methods," they make it clear that combining different epistemologies is "not our intent" (Barkin and Sjoberg 2015a; Sjoberg 2015: 1007). A similar line of thinking is also found in Hutchings' (2011) discussion regarding dialogue beyond "the West/non-West distinction." She points to the importance of "dialogue as conversation," which presupposes little about who or how many are speaking, in contrast to dialogue as "a kind of negotiation," which inevitably involves subsumption or synthesis in favour of the powerful.

In short, the call for more engagement and dialogue across theories should not be read as a call for unity. Instead, it is a call for a clear indication of the strengths of each perspective and where the various perspectives' research interests (can) overlap and thus complement each other.

In order to meet this goal, it is first necessary to clarify and expand points of contact and common reference between "isms" – that is, between (neo)positivism and post-positivism (or between "rationalism" and "reflectivism," to borrow Keohane's term). Here, methodology and methods, particularly in post-positivist contexts, can serve as useful points of contact, for three reasons.

Incommensurability

The first reason is relatively straightforward: it is not methodology or methods per se, but philosophical stances that give rise to the alleged incommensurability between competing "isms" and what Lake (2011: 465) refers to as "academic sectarianism," which engages in "self-affirming research and then wage[s] theological debates." In the history of IR, the "great debates" and theoretical divides have largely revolved around fundamental differences in terms of philosophical (namely, ontological and/or epistemological) positions. For example: What is the world made of? Is there a "mind-independent" world (Jackson 2011)? What do we mean by "scientific" research (Neumann 2014)? Can we have any "knowledge beyond the realm of experience" (Suganami 2013: 254)? That the answers to such philosophical questions have been so disparate has contributed significantly to the impasse in the debates in IR; in the ongoing (third or fourth) debate, in particular, the issue of incommensurability revolves around ontological and/or epistemological issues – for instance, assumptions about objectivity and subjectivity and the role and function of science (Wæver 1996: 156–157). In their influential *Explaining and Understanding International Relations*, Martin Hollis and Steve Smith argue that there are always (at least) "two stories" to tell about international relations – because of the mutually "irreconcilable" philosophical underpinnings embedded in our debates about world politics (Hollis and Smith 1990: 211, 215). Viewed in this light, the problem of incommensurability between positivism and post-positivism is likely to remain unresolved.

However, it is important to note here that incommensurability is a result of differences at the level of philosophy or metatheory, and not at a methodological level. Methodology and methods *can* travel across the boundaries set by ontology or epistemology more easily than is generally recognised. For example, although IR has a tendency to pair a certain group of methods (e.g. quantitative methods) with a certain metatheoretical position (e.g. positivism), this pairing is not cast in stone. Further, such a limited pairing is not only unnecessary, but also hinders our ability to understand international relations, as Samuel Barkin and Laura Sjoberg's (2017) edited volume demonstrates. Obviously, ontology, epistemology, and methodology are closely related: Marsh and Furlong (2002: 21) assert that the relationship between ontology, epistemology, and methodology is like "a skin, not a sweater that can be put on when we are addressing philosophical issues and taken off when we are doing political research." But this does not suggest that the use of methodologies and methods should be subordinated to a certain ontological or epistemological position. Even if the boundaries and gaps between "isms" are rigid and wide, thus making dialogue difficult, this difficulty is located mainly at the level of metatheory. A constructive and interesting engagement can indeed take place at the level of methodology and methods. They are able to provide opportunities for IR researchers working within "isms" to explore the potential (or previously unrecognised) similarities and "overlaps" between paradigms and thus realise the benefits of further interaction and dialogue.

For example, critical theorists who do not accept the problem-solving epistemology of positivism could (and, to a certain extent, need to) employ positivist *methods* because the critical nature of their theory is in effect produced by a "reflexive recognition" of social and political worlds that is necessarily "based on an *empirical* assessment" of how social and political realities are produced and evolve throughout history (Hamati-Ataya 2013: 681–682, emphasis added).[2] Once critical theorists realise that their research can benefit from methodological tools they have ignored or rejected on the basis of metatheoretical commitments, greater interaction and engagement are likely to result. In brief, if anything is likely to be a candidate for promoting dialogue between theoretical paradigms, it is methodology and methods, rather than ontology and epistemology, for the former can avoid the issue of the irresolvability of basic philosophical issues while playing a substantive role in finding, constituting, and expanding points of contact and common reference in a divided IR.

The logic that method(ology), as opposed to metatheory, can serve as an effective platform on which dialogue across competing paradigms can be facilitated seems to be at play in the promotion of "global dialogue" in IR beyond the West/non-West distinction. Consider, for instance, the recent comments by Yan Xuetong, who is well known for his strong advocacy of "Chinese IR" as an alternative to Western-(American-)centric IR. In an interview with a Western IR journal, where he discusses "Chinese realism" and the Chinese "Tsinghua School" of IR, he makes the following comments:

> I think there are two major thinkers that matter [for Chinese IR] here: Qin Yaqing and Zhao Tingyang. Actually I think there is some similarity between Qin Yaqing and myself, and what Qin and me share is that we do not have a connection with Zhao Tingyang.
> (Xuetong, cited in Creutzfeldt 2012: 3)

Xuetong offers an interesting answer to why that is the case:

> Zhao is a *philosopher* and his books are about *philosophy*, rather than about the real world. … As for Qin, we are very close. … For instance, his method of study is also very scientific; both of us use the scientific *method*. On that basis, it is easy for us to communicate with each other.
> (Xuetong, cited in Creutzfeldt 2012: 3–4, emphasis added)

In other words, despite the fact that Yan Xuetong's thoughts are different from those of Qin Yaqing (e.g. in terms of the unit of analysis), he believes that the use of a similar research method enables them to engage in dialogue with each other.

As discussed earlier, there is also a strong commitment to (positivist) *methods* in other Asian IR communities, including Japan and South Korea. Although Asian IR has persistently attempted to build indigenous IR theories, such endeavours have been carried out with a belief that Asia has distinctive ontologies, not methodologies, made up of unique cultural practices, histories, and traditions. Asian IR communities commonly highlight the significance of "method" even in the case of establishing an indigenous IR theory. The ways in which theory is built, tested, and eventually accepted or rejected is a matter of great concern to both advocates and critics in the discussion of "non-Western" IR theory building in the Chinese, Japanese, and Korean IR communities (Song 2001; Choi 2008; Yamamoto 2011; Chen 2011). Of course, this is not to say that method (ology) is the sole means through which to promote dialogue between theoretical (and spatial) divides, but only that dialogue is easier in the realm of method(ology) than in the realms of ontology or epistemology.

Points of contact

The second reason why it is useful to focus on methodology and methods is based on a more practical consideration of the existing norm regarding knowledge production in IR. Methodology and methods "have increasingly been placed at the heart" of IR scholarship in terms of both research and publishing, on the one hand, and teaching practices, on the other (Aradau and Huysmans 2014: 597; see also Yanow and Schwartz-Shea 2010). This is mainly because methodology and methods are treated as the most important criteria by which to judge competing knowledge claims. In fact, as Lawrence Mead argues, methodological advice and standards are seen as indispensable components of any actually existing line of "scientific" research across the entire discipline of political science, including IR (Mead 2010: 454). In addition, the currently "dominant" methodological position in IR is held (or has been "usurped," to use Roy Bhaskar's word) by (neo)positivism, which, whether we like it or not, has very clear and specific methodological principles and procedures, such as hypothesis testing with statistical techniques (Jackson 2015: 13). For example, Gary King, Robert Keohane, and Sidney Verba's *Designing Social Inquiry* is firmly grounded in a *positivist* understanding of what the "scientific" study of world politics should entail. *Designing Social Inquiry* conceives the goal of "scientific" research as "inference," arguing that we should make inferential claims from empirical observations based on the rules and methods developed in the context of statistical analysis. Going a step further, King et al. hold that "the logic of good qualitative and good quantitative research designs do not fundamentally differ," in the sense that a "unified" (positivist) *method* of inference can and should be applied to both (King et al. 1994: vii–3).

In short, here "good," "scientific" research is defined in positivist *methodological* terms. As David Lake writes, "there is now substantial agreement on the basic methodology of and standards for positivist social-scientific research" (Lake 2013: 578–579). Consider, for example, the fact that statistical analysis, hypothesis testing, and data manipulation have become indispensable requirements of all IR methodological courses at universities (Hagmann and Biersteker 2014). Given this existing disciplinary norm of IR, which foregrounds methodology and methods in the process of knowledge production, as well as positivist scholars' serious and persistent concerns with them, it is necessary for post-positivists to pay greater attention to methodology and especially methods in order to create more opportunities for dialogue. Again, this is not to suggest that methodology or methods should be prioritised in the study of world politics or that a commitment to positivist methods associated with empirical evaluation is all IR needs in order to locate itself on "scientific" ground. What it does imply is that given the methodology-centred norm underlying the process of knowledge production in the field, active post-positivist engagement in methodology and methods can constitute useful *points of contact* in IR.

Unfortunately, however, there is a relative lack of concern with or discussion of methodological issues in post-positivist research; methodology and especially methods tend to be spoken of either vaguely or negatively within post-positivist scholarship. In Iver B. Neumann's words,

> In IR, the discipline's quantitative practitioners are passionate about the problems surrounding data programming, in such a degree that one sometimes wonders if counting is not being substituted for thinking, but at least the quants do engage in a debate about methods. Those of us who mostly do qualitative stuff, however, must be severely faulted for having largely neglected methods.
>
> (Neumann 2014: 337–338)

To be sure, there have been several meaningful and important attempts by post-positivist IR scholars to address methodological questions. These include Jennifer Milliken's widely cited piece on discourse analysis (Milliken 1999); Lene Hansen's work considering "intertextuality" as the methodological core of the critical study of security and foreign policy (Hansen 2006); Brooke Ackerly, Maria Stern, and Jacqui True's edited volume on feminist IR methodologies highlighting "reflexivity" of the self (Ackerly et al. 2006); Vincent Pouliot's "sobjectivism" as a constructivist methodology (Pouliot 2007); and, more recently, Claudia Aradau and Jef Huysmans' (2014) article on the roles and political functions of methods in the discipline. These studies are exceptions, however. Furthermore, on closer examination, post-positivist IR studies on methodology, despite their contributions, tend to treat methodological issues as subordinate to the philosophical and normative stances they advocate.[3] Let me clarify these points further.

Generally speaking, post-positivist IR scholarship remains sceptical about actively engaging in methodology. Methodology and methods tend to be considered as "at best touched upon in the opening pages of monographs" (Neumann 2014: 338). In effect, as Aradau and Huysmans (2014: 600) observe, there is a strong tendency in post-positivist IR scholarship to see method(ology) as a "disciplining" tool "tainted by the allegation of positivism." For this reason, many post-positivist IR scholars have "privileged ontology and epistemology ... at the expense of methodology. [...] Despite other differences, constructivist, post-structuralist, feminist, and critical realist scholars would largely agree on this move towards ontology and/or epistemology *contra* ... method" (Aradau and Huysmans 2014: 600, 597).

In this context, post-positivist discussions about methodology and methods are often subsumed or trapped within metatheory; the idea that ontology or epistemology comes first is commonly found in post-positivist IR research. Consider, for example, Pouliot's argument for "sobjectivism," Colin Wight's discussion of the "agent-structure problem" in IR, or Ackerly, Stern, and True's work on "feminist IR": although they all discuss methodology, they do so on the terrain of metatheory, as if methodology only functioned or existed in relation to certain ontological or epistemological positions. More specifically, what Ackerly et al. (2006: 4–10) intend to search for is methodological tools commensurate with their epistemological commitments based on feminist understandings of knowledge and politics.[4] Going a step further, Wight (2006: 259) argues that "[m]ethodologies are always, or at least should be, ontologically specific." Put simply, the main concerns of post-positivist IR research lie in philosophical rather than methodological issues, where the chances of bringing about dialogue are slim.[5] The bottom line is that *more exceptions* to these trends – namely, a shortage of discussion of methodology and methods and a "metatheoretically bounded" approach to the discussion of methodological issues – are required to generate more dialogue in IR.

Translating metatheoretical insights into empirical knowledge

Closely related to this point is my third reason. I suggest that post-positivists need to dedicate more intellectual resources to methodology and methods in order to clarify how their *metatheoretical* insights lead to different types of *empirical* knowledge. It seems that even in the few post-positivist IR studies that place methodology firmly at the heart of the work, there is a serious lack of discussion or concrete examples of how their insights and suggestions can be translated into empirical knowledge, and with what kinds of methods. For example, Aradau and Huysmans' recent work, despite its special emphasis on the "critical" role of "methods," attempts to reconceptualise methods as "political devices which enact worlds and acts which disrupt particular worlds" (2014: 598), but without explaining how this reconceptualisation is translated into empirical knowledge or connected with the fabric of "empiry." I think that methodologies *tailored for* ontological, epistemological, or normative positions favoured by post-positivist paradigms are not sufficient to induce dialogue and engagement in IR, a divided field in which positivist, empirical methodologies remain central. Rather, there is a need for post-positivist scholarship to offer specific and explicit methodological guidelines on how to traverse the bridge that connects the insights of their favoured ontologies or epistemologies to empirical research and knowledge.

In the disciplinary history of IR, there has been long-standing "scepticism about the relevance of post-positivist IR to empirical research" (Hamati-Ataya 2013: 670; see also Keohane 1988). As such, reducing this scepticism is not only useful, but also necessary. As already explained, methodology and methods are at the centre of attention and practice in the field (at least in the mainstream IR paradigm); and what "scientific" research of international relations should entail is frequently conceived of in a methodological sense as intimately tied to *empirical* analysis and evaluation. As Christian Reus-Smit (2013: 604) observes, "[t]raditionally, mainstream International Relations scholars (and political scientists) confined the field to empirical-theoretic inquiry on [positivist] epistemological principle. ... The tenuous nature of this position is now widely acknowledged by mainstream scholars." Even analytical eclecticism, which draws insights from multiple theoretical perspectives, is intrinsically an "empirical-theoretic" project. Rudra Sil and Peter J. Katzenstein, who have long argued for analytical eclecticism, emphasise the complementarity or intersection of empirical puzzles identified by contending paradigms. In their words, an eclectic approach aims "to recognise and evaluate what is going on in different research traditions concerned with different aspects of problems ... in *empirical* terms" (Sil and Katzenstein 2010: 415, emphasis added). Put simply, analytical eclecticism – which "has quite rapidly become part of mainstream debates about the kind of knowledge the field ought to pursue" (Reus-Smit 2013: 604; Wight 2013: 327) – is intended to address empirical puzzles and produce empirical knowledge. Viewed in this light, discussing and practicing methodology and methods in post-positivist contexts with the aim of generating different types of empirical knowledge could spark considerable interest and attention among IR scholars, including sceptics of post-positivist thinking; this could in turn motivate positivists to listen more carefully to their counterparts.

An important point that needs emphasis here is that positivists rarely initiate dialogue. As J. Ann Tickner (2011: 609, 611) puts it, they (as the "winners") have "rarely been willing to engage losers" in a series of "debates" in the disciplinary history of IR. Even if the "losers" show great interest in dialogue, it is "not reciprocated by the mainstream" as long as those interests remain at the level of metatheory. In order to initiate much-needed dialogue between positivist and post-positivist paradigms, therefore, methodology needs to be taken more seriously by post-positivist scholarship. As such, what is advocated here should not be seen as a subordinative approach to dialogue.

Furthermore, the employment of empirical methods in addressing post-positivist questions can be considered a useful way of connecting post-positivist insights at a philosophical level to knowledge at the level of empiry (and thereby promoting dialogue between "isms"). For example, in order to achieve human "emancipation," which is the main concern of critical theory, an "empirically grounded assessment" of the evolution of social systems and how social actors are involved in the evolution (i.e. production and reproduction) of meaning is necessary (Hamati-Ataya 2013: 688; Devetak 2014); statistics can play an important and useful role in providing "the empirical basis for theoretical arguments, whether those arguments themselves are positivist or not" (Barkin and Sjoberg 2015b: 13). Also, Hayward Alker (1996) has shown that post-structuralist research can make use of mathematics and modelling in highly innovative ways, challenging commonsensical understandings of their "scientific" functions. In addition, as Barkin and Sjoberg's (2017) book demonstrates, critical and constructivist IR research can benefit from the use of quantitative, formal, and computational methods: Sjoberg and Knudson's (2017) chapter, in particular, demonstrates that the tools of geometric and computational topology are very useful in carrying out concept mapping for critical theorising in IR.[6]

In addition, the prospective benefits of post-positivists' more active engagement with empirical forms of methodology and methods include not only interactive debates across the theoretical divide in IR, but also the development of post-positivist IR scholarship. As long as post-positivism remains in the realm of metatheory, it can neither produce the type of alternative theory with which post-positivist scholars hope to replace positivism nor dynamically contribute to the socio-historical knowledge of the world. In this regard, Inanna Hamati-Ataya's (2013: 681–682) observation is worthy of note. In her discussion of the core concept of a critical IR, namely "reflexivity," she comments as follows:

> Surely, reflexivity itself must *result from* an empirical assessment of *whether/how* knowledge is subtended by "politico-normative" or "ideological" principles. Reflexivity is therefore necessarily *produced by* and *productive of* empirical knowledge. [...] The move from meta-theory ... to empiry is therefore *logically* and *praxically* necessary for critical IR.

She adds that one way of moving to empiry is by translating "reflexivity into a methodology for empirical social science" (Hamati-Ataya 2013:

681–682, emphasis added). Although she does not go into detail about how to engage in this translation, the point she makes is clear: there is a need for a sophisticated post-positivist methodology for empirical research in IR. Sharing this concern, several critical IR theorists have highlighted the practical meaning of reflexivity for empirical IR (see, e.g., Guzzini 2005; Lynch 2008; Ackerly and True 2008).

In this regard, what Steve Smith wrote more than a decade ago is still pertinent: "the acid test for the success of alternative and critical approaches is the extent to which they have led to empirically grounded work that explores the range and variety of world politics" (Smith 2002: 202). Nonetheless, as Gerard van der Ree (2013: 42) writes, methods of knowledge representation and production associated with numbers, modelling, and mathematics are "generally evaded in post-modern, post-structural, and critical scholarship." With respect to this trend, van der Ree goes on to argue that "to unreflexively disregard numbers and mathematics (which are in themselves languages) in an attempt to escape knowledge hierarchies seems to throw out the baby with the bathwater" (van der Ree (2013: 42) In other words, in evading numbers and mathematics, post-positivists forfeit a valuable opportunity to develop a more nuanced and reflexive understanding of the "disciplinary" functions and roles of numbers and mathematics within the discipline, such as the relationships between numerical knowledge representation and the so-called "science question." This in turn allows positivist scholarship to claim numbers and mathematics as legitimate sources of authority; as a result, debates between positivists and post-positivists remain based on stereotypes and/or misunderstandings.

In summary, if post-positive IR scholarship considered methodology in its own right and not as subordinate to ontology or epistemology, and if it employed the methods associated with empirical knowledge production more fully, a space for active dialogue would be created. This shift could in turn lead to IR becoming a more dialogical discipline.

To re-emphasise, this is not to suggest that (positivist) methodology or methods should be prioritised in international studies, but only that more dialogue in IR requires, at a minimum, the active engagement of post-positivists in methodological issues. Relatedly, what is advocated here should not be interpreted as an absolute endorsement of the empirical methods favoured by positivist analysts. To say that methodology and (empirical) methods can be useful points of contact in IR is not to argue for positivism as such. As mentioned at the outset of this chapter, methodology and methods are a means for the production and advancement of knowledge of international relations, not ends in themselves. We must *first* talk to each other. Only through vigorous dialogue can we realise more clearly when each approach offers greater insights and, more importantly, where the research concerns of the various approaches can "overlap" and thus produce complementary understandings of the complex reality underlying world politics. Put differently, without dialogue, the expansion of knowledge is likely to remain limited, for it is neither easy to identify one's own blind spots nor feasible to make our critiques of other approaches heard unless we talk to each other.

If methodology and methods are seen as effective devices for seeing ourselves in others and seeing others in ourselves rather than as a "disciplining" tool used to judge the "scientificity" of knowledge, then scepticism about these issues harboured by many post-positivist (particularly postmodern) IR researchers could be reduced and the motivation to engage in methodological questions might be increased. Hence, method(ology), which seems to remain at the margins of post-positivist IR scholarship, deserves renewed attention as a point of *contact and dialogue* between the positivist and post-positivist paradigms.

An example will help clarify what such dialogue could look like, and is especially relevant given the tendency for those who argue for a post-positivist research programme that foregrounds empirical analysis to neither provide specific methodological guidelines nor give concrete illustrations with respect to how to do so (for a similar critique, see Harvey and Cobb 2003: 145).

I focus on the example of Critical Realism (CR) and offer methodological guidelines for its empirical analysis. I have chosen CR because it has raised major metatheoretical issues in our discipline (Patomäki 2002; Wight 2006; Kurki 2008; Joseph and Wight 2010) and because a main criticism of CR is that it is not concerned with methodological issues (see, e.g., Hall 2009; Lebow 2011: 1226).

The following methodological discussion is by no means exhaustive or comprehensive in scope (for essential readings on CR, see Archer et al. 1998). Nonetheless, I trust that, despite its necessary brevity, it will be useful in demonstrating the importance of active engagement in methodology and methods among post-positivists, especially in relation to empirical analysis, for generating greater dialogue across the positivist–post-positivist divide.

An illustration: Critical Realism in methodological practice

CR is the movement in philosophy, the human sciences, and cognate practices most closely associated with the work of Roy Bhaskar. It attempts to transcend the dichotomy between "a hyper-naturalistic positivism and an anti-naturalistic hermeneutics" (Archer et al. 1998, ix–xiii). The core assumptions of CR regarding causation and the nature of social reality can be summarised as follows: causes exist as (ontologically) real forces in the world around us ("nothing comes from nothing"); the social world is an open system; causes in the social world are often unobservable; and society "is not the unconditioned creation of human agents but neither does it exist independently of it ... and individual action neither completely determines nor is completely determined by social forms" (Bhaskar 1982: 286).

On the basis of these ontological premises, CR claims that both human agents and social structures – that is, both agential and structural (ideational and material) factors and elements – are necessary for any social act to be possible, since they are ontologically real objects (causes for actions) and are interlinked: every social act, event, or phenomenon is only possible insofar as the structural contexts/conditions for action and the agents who act exist.

CR has several implications for IR. For example, a state's foreign policy behaviours can be understood as resulting from a dynamic process in which human agents (e.g. policymakers) and the structural conditions within which they act causally affect each other. More specifically, while foreign policies are indeed made by policymakers and thus reflect their core beliefs about political and social life, policymakers' capacity to create policies is determined (constrained and/or facilitated) by the structural conditions of the world in which they find themselves – geography, international norms, and the distribution of material power, for example. A CR study of international relations assumes that the causes of the state's behaviour in world politics can be both structural and agential in both the material and ideational senses and, thus, argues that the concept of causation should be liberated from "the deterministic and mechanistic connotations that it has in much of International Relations scholarship" (Kurki 2008: 11). In short, CR posits that agential and structural factors always come together in complex and non-predetermined ways, and it criticises the positivist understanding of causation, which it perceives as "regularity-determinism" (Bhaskar 1978, 70), for being too narrow and thus unable to adequately explain states' behaviour.

Methodologically, then, it follows that CR adopts methodological pluralism, in contrast to the positivist emphasis on quantitative methods and the interpretive emphasis on qualitative methods (Kurki and Wight 2013: 27). According to Critical Realists, the question of whether material factors or ideational issues are the most important in determining outcomes is an empirical matter; and this only can be decided through an examination of the relationship and interplay of both. As such, analysts must be open to both quantitative and qualitative methods and data. Methodologically, this suggests that IR researchers concerned with why-questions about state behaviour should employ a multicausal and open-ended approach in which the causal status of both structural and agential (material and ideational) factors are accepted and the relative causal effects of the chosen factors are not predetermined. The methodological position discussed here can simply be referred to as an open-ended multicausal approach. Whether the factors chosen can in fact explain an observed phenomenon must be determined empirically. Consequently, IR researchers who seek to understand what really happened – in other words, to determine causation and not just correlation – must examine whether the causal capacities of the chosen factors have been activated by engaging in both a quantitative and qualitative empirical investigation of the explanatory weight of the factors, using both hard and soft data. We must then reconstruct the causal processes of the observed phenomenon with the factors that receive empirical support.

This may sound complicated, but a multicausal and open-ended approach is manageable if a method of isolation and exclusion is employed. For example, suppose that we are puzzled as to why a particular nation (e.g. the United States) embarked on a given external action (e.g. going to war against Iraq) and that we assume that the political beliefs of key policymakers (e.g. George W. Bush) were one of the reasons. While isolating – or, in Anthony Giddens' (1979, 80) words, "bracketing" off[7] – the other potential causal factors for the moment, we must examine the explanatory strength of the chosen factor. In order to do so, we first need to infer the subject's (Bush's) political beliefs through a close investigation of his public and/or private statements – for example, speeches, interviews, press conferences – which display his views on the nature of political and social life (for classic illustrations of this method, see Holsti 1962, 1967). Having inferred his political beliefs, we will be able to discern whether the causal capacity of Bush's political beliefs was activated – that is, whether the subject's political beliefs can explain the phenomenon in question. This is, in Alexander George's terminology, the "congruence procedure" (George 1969; for subsequent research, see, e.g., Young and Schafer 1998; Schafer and Walker 2006; Renshon 2008). And if the test confirms the explanatory power, then the chosen factor (Bush's political beliefs) becomes an indispensable *part* of the cause of the observed phenomenon (the decision by the United States to go to war against Iraq). But if the investigation indicates that political beliefs do not have significant explanatory weight, then they are set aside and other potential factors, for instance states' material interests, are considered.

This way of reasoning enables the observer to discern the causes of an observed phenomenon and reconstruct its causal processes in a systemic and clear manner. I describe the method put forward here as a logical process in which multiple causes are found by employing a flexible epistemological and methodological approach that stands on a rich ontological platform formulated prior to application of the approach. More simply, it can be referred to as a loose-knit deductive reasoning method.[8]

To be sure, I am not saying that the methodological guidelines for applying CR to an empirical analysis of states' actions are uncontroversial. Nor am I suggesting that they will solve all empirical or conceptual puzzles connected to world political processes and phenomena. I admit that the methodological scheme has shortcomings: for instance, a multicausal and open-ended approach is laborious; it appears to be an "inelegant" alternative to more parsimonious models; and it has many loose ends in comparison to rigorous deductive approaches that establish a firm link between a small number of operative variables with the aim of making or discovering universal generalisations.

At the same time, these limitations should not obscure the fundamental points put forward in this chapter. It is through methodology and methods that we can achieve deeper engagement and more dialogue across IR perspectives; and post-positivists in particular need to pay greater attention to discussing and, more importantly, practicing methods through which different types of empirical knowledge can be harvested. Although such efforts may lead to another contentious and exhausting round of debate, it is a challenge worth taking if our goal is to produce vigorous dialogue across the enduring positivist–post-positivist divide. When post-positivist scholarship confronts, develops, and practices – rather than denies, avoids, and marginalises – methodology and especially empirical methods, it facilitates dialogue in the discipline.

Notes

1 Of course, there are exceptions. Alexander Wendt's latest attempt to unify physical and social ontology based on "quantum consciousness theory" and Andrew Bennett's persistent call for "middle-ground" epistemologies are probably two of the most prominent and recent examples (see Wendt 2015; Bennett 2015).
2 This point is discussed further later on in this chapter.
3 There are some exceptions, including Alker (1996) and Sjoberg and Horowitz (2013).

4 A similar line of thinking is found in J. Ann Tickner's (2005) "So What Is Your Research Program? Some Feminist Answers to International Relations Methodological Questions."

5 Again, recall the existing disciplinary norm of IR, which foregrounds methodology and methods in the production of knowledge.

6 I would like to thank Samuel and Laura for sharing their insights regarding their book with me.

7 Although Giddens introduced this terminology, he has been criticised for his lack of concern with methodological issues by a number of commentators (see, e.g., Thrift 1985; Cohen 1989). The problem is simply that Giddens does not give sufficient examples or guidelines for operationalising his concept of "bracketing." Critics often note that he needs to explicate how bracketing could and should be applied in empirical analyses (see, e.g., Thrift 1985; Poole and DeSanctis 2004; Kort and Gharbi 2013: 98–99).

8 For a detailed exposition of this method and the metatheoretical rationales underlying it, see Eun (2012).

5   Broadening IR through dialogue
Interweaving Western IR theory with
the indigenous experience of Asia

How can we promote "global dialogue" in IR beyond the West/non-West distinction? At the same time as interest in "non-Western" IR has been increasing, concerns about the West/non-West divide have arisen in international studies. In other words, the various "non-Western" IR projects (be they "non-Western," "post-Western," or "Global" IR) inevitably raise concerns about fragmentation in the field. The issue of theoretical diversity and fragmentation needs to be subject to much greater critical scrutiny than it has hitherto received. This is so because, although our persistent calls for more diversity in IR theory appear relatively unproblematic or straightforward, the issues at stake are not so simple. For example, the more diversity IR has, the greater the number of dividing lines that are likely to emerge in the field; and the emergence of dividing lines would lead the already divided discipline of IR to what Oren (2016: 571) calls a "fragmented adhocracy," which is a hindrance to knowledge accumulation and thus progress in IR. This is a main reason that some IR scholars take issue with pluralism. Brian Schmidt (2008: 108, emphasis added) notes as follows:

> too much pluralism leaves us with a divided discipline that not only fails to speak with one voice, but cannot even agree on what we should be studying, focusing on, or seeking to explain. Pluralism, in other words, masks the fact that we have an *incoherent* field.

A similar critique is also made by Michael Brecher and Frank Harvey in their reflexive study of contemporary IR theory. Exhibiting a deep concern about the lack of progress and knowledge accumulation in the field, they write that alternative and critical perspectives in IR "encompass an array of research programs and findings that are not easily grouped into a common set of beliefs, theories or conclusions ... [and thus have] difficulty agreeing on what they have accomplished"

(Brecher and Harvey 2002: 2) That is, although the theoretical terrain of contemporary IR has become much wider since the late 1980s (Rengger 2015; Eun 2016), the theoretical proliferation has also "no doubt produced monadic communities unable and unwilling to communicate with one another" (Pasha 2011: 685).

In response, scholars advocating for a broadening of IR – particularly in the name of "Global" IR – often suggest that IR should engage in more active "dialogue" and "engagement" across growing theoretical and spatial divides. Andrew Hurrell (2016: 150), for example, notes that "Global IR" should aim to have "a far broader conversation that uncovers the production of differently situated accounts, narratives, and stories about the global and its associated and related ideas and concepts." What these scholars call for is not to discard or disavow Western-centric IR, but rather to render it broader and more inclusive so that more diversity and more dialogue are brought about and thus voices and experiences outside of the West are reflected more fully. Acharya (2014: 649) makes this point clear by saying that "while one cannot and should not seek to displace existing (or future) theories of IR that may substantially originate from Western ideas and experiences, it is possible, through dialogue and discovery, to build alternative theories ... that have their origin in the South." Later he adds: "encouraging debate and dialogue across perspectives ... is a core purpose of the Global IR project" (Acharya 2016: 14).

This call for dialogue, again, superficially appears unproblematic and undisputed, but things are not so simple. As Kimberly Hutchings aptly notes, dialogue can be a mere exchange or encounter that is already "staged and scripted" by the mainstream (namely, in the case of IR, the West and positivists); in this respect, it could turn out to be "a piece of rhetorical bullying" (Hutchings 2011: 645). Furthermore, a "staged and scripted" dialogue across theories can lead to an inward-looking tug of war between rival camps over truth claims, which in turn impedes progress in the discipline. David Lake (2013), in this sense, suggests that IR ought to pursue working *within* paradigms rather than working *across* paradigms. In his words, "The field would be better off ... achieving progress within each approach according to its own criteria for success. [...] This suggests letting each paradigm develop on its own in its own fashion" (Lake 2013: 567, 580).

Despite these concerns, many IR scholars, including Hutchings and Lake, do not oppose dialogue per se. Indeed, "vigorous" debates across cultures and regions and active engagement from alternative theoretical perspectives are frequently promoted by proponents of a broader IR. This is also the case in reflexive discussions regarding the prospects of

IR theory, as discussed in Chapter 4. The "integrative pluralism" advanced by Tim Dunne, Lene Hansen, and Colin Wight is a representative case in point. In their piece titled "The End of International Relations Theory?" they argue that IR should move towards "integrative pluralism" in which not only diversity, but more importantly "engagement" across competing theoretical paradigms is encouraged (Dunne et al. 2013a: 416–417). In a related vein, Patrick Jackson also foregrounds "engaged pluralism," which "brings unlike elements into dialogue with one another without fusing them into a specious synthesis" as a way of advancing IR (Jackson 2011: 207). More than a decade ago, Yosef Lapid proposed that if "pluralism ... is the most feasible and deserving destination for the international relations theory enterprise in the foreseeable future, then dialogue must figure prominently on our agenda at the dawn of the twenty-first century" (Lapid 2003: 129). In short, the importance of dialogue in a pluralistic but divided IR is readily acknowledged in the IR literature.

A critical question then is how we can ensure proper dialogue and engagement across theoretical divides without descending to a narcissistic turf war. This question is timely in that IR is an *already* divided and fragmented discipline (Lake 2013). It is also a very important question from the perspective of the "broadening" IR project in that what it aims to achieve could increase divisions and fragmentation unless meaningful dialogue between existing (Western-centric) IR theories and alternative (or indigenous) understandings occurs. Although those concerned with theoretical fragmentation and parochialism persistently call for active dialogue across theoretical and geopolitical divides, they do not elaborate how we could achieve this goal. As a result, "dialogue, a persistent dream in IR, remains elusive, recurrent cycles of small openings followed by closure" (Pasha 2011: 684). To be sure, there are a few important exceptions (Hutchings 2011; Bilgin 2016), but they remain just that – exceptions.

In the following section, I offer illustrations to discuss the ways in which dialogue can be promoted across the West/non-West divide. The focus here is on dialogue and mutual learning between Western-centric IR and Asian regional politics, more specifically between constructivist IR theory and the foreign policy and local history of East Asian states.

Illustrations: A move towards dialogue between Western-centric IR theory and indigenous knowledge of East Asia

Most scholars agree that socially constructed attributes, such as national identity and nationalism, matter a great deal in East Asian international relations. IR and area studies have a wealth of literature advocating this view. According to constructivism, for example, social and ideational attributes form our conceptions of who we are and what we value; they in turn define the content of states' interests and therefore the way they "act" in global politics (Wendt 1994, 1999). It is "identity" that constructs "a particular set of interests or preferences with respect to choices of action" in international politics (Hopf 1998: 175). Drawing on these constructivist insights, scholars interested in East Asian regional politics observe that "nationalism appears to be rising in a renascent Asia, stoking tensions, aspirations, pride, and identity politics" (Kingston 2015: 1). Shin (2015: 189) notes that "historical memories and national identity" shape Northeast Asian inter-state relations. Going a step further, Zheng Wang (2013: 16) claims that "different inter-pretations of history and differences in identity … must be seen as a cause for conflict" between China and Japan. In this respect, concerned scholars suggest that East Asia narrow "the gaps in the perceptions of identity" through "historical reconciliation" so as to improve regional cooperation (Kwak and Nobles 2013: 4). Further, these claims lead to the following analytical injunction: one needs to pay great attention to national identity or historical memory in order to make sense of the present and future of East Asian international politics (Rozman 2012; Arai et al. 2013; Kim 2015; Glosserman and Snyder 2015).

Despite the voluminous literature on the importance of national identity and its implications for East Asian international politics, the questions of *how* and *to what extent* this ideational and social construct matters in the foreign policies of East Asian countries remain unclear or under-explored. An attempt to answer these questions requires both theoretical and empirical knowledge. That is, we need theoretical knowledge regarding the causal mechanisms and processes of national identity in relation to a state's foreign policy *and* empirical observation of how national identity actually plays a causal role in the foreign policy actions of East Asian countries. Unfortunately, however, it is often acknowledged that area studies on Asia lack the former (i.e. theoretical and methodological commitments to an understanding of causal mechanisms) and that theoretical IR studies do not pay due attention to the latter (i.e. empirical, local knowledge of individual Asian countries' foreign policy). In effect, the two fields remain dis-parate, although both acknowledge the importance of national iden-tity. Hence, this is a point where dialogue and mutual learning can and should take place. In other words, our attempts to answer *how* and *to what extent* national identity matters in East Asian foreign relations can contribute to achieving an inclusive IR in which active dialogue across differently situated theories, histories, and locations takes place.

To demonstrate this, I first undertake a theoretical review of how national identity develops. Then I carry out an empirical analysis, using South Korea as a case study. The focus here is on identifying the roots of South Korean national identity and examining whether and how it has worked in practice as a cause of its actual foreign policy behaviour vis-à-vis Japan and North Korea.

National identity: What it is and how it is formed

While scholars may define the term in slightly different ways, national identity is a collective belief, shared by individuals belonging to the same nation, that they are historically, ethnically, culturally, and politically related. These individuals often feel a sense of solidarity with other individuals, past and present, who are members of the same nation. More specifically, Anthony Smith (1991: 11) defines national identity as "a set of common understandings and aspirations, sentiments and ideas ... that bind the population together in their homeland." Similarly, William Bloom (1993: 18) understands national identity as "a particular set of cultural mores and political norms ... passed down from generation to generation" that form the "collective self" for "a particular ethnos." Since national identity, in Guibernau's words (2004: 135), "reflects the sentiment of belonging to the nation" over generations, it is intrinsic in the socialisation of individuals. That is, national identity is transmitted "across generational lines by processes of education and acculturation" (Friedberg 2005: 34). "Acculturation," of course, refers to the process by which individuals internalise cultural, social, and political norms (Bloom 1993, 52). This process forms and consolidates a "collective identification" (Wendt 1994: 386).

The process of "collective identification" necessitates a corresponding process of differentiation or dissociation from individuals who are not members of the nation. To preserve the social coherence, solidarity, and uniqueness of the nation, it is necessary to cast non-members as "others." One of the two key elements that define any national identity is the concept of "difference" from others (Campbell 1992: 2–8). A nation's myths or traditions are often "powerful differentiators and reminders of the unique culture and fate of the ethnic community" (Guibernau 2004: 126; see also Smith 1998). As Duncan Bell (2003: 67) sums up neatly, "representation and recognition of us and them act as the mutually supporting scaffolds upon which national identity is constructed." All national identities must answer both the question "who are we?" and the question "who are they?" to provide a coherent world view.

There are several attributes, including territory, language, religion, cultural values, and traditions, that give the members of a nation a sense of solidarity; and shared historical memories and myths are often considered the most potent tools with which to define "us" and "them" (Bell 2003; Campbell 1992; Poole 1999; Smith 1986, 1991). This is so because "basically, a nation is a group of people who feel that they are *ancestrally* related" (Guibernau 2004: 135, emphasis in original) and because "nation-building" is a "historical" process (Smith 1991: 13). Scholars commonly acknowledge that instead of some predetermined entity, the nation is a "social construction, fluid in content, whose meaning is determined by historical contexts" (Weiner 1997: xii). Historical context and meaningful group experiences can alter the collective values that make up national identity. Bloom (1993: 52) argues that "a shared group identification can be triggered only by meaningful and real historical experience." Recent studies in the field of social psychology confirm that a nation's collective experiences and memories engender national coherence as well as contributing to national perceptions of the "self" and "other" (Vertzberger 2005; Pennebaker et al. 2013).

Understanding the historical experience of a particular nation is, then, key to understanding the identity of that nation. Jenny Edkins (2003: 45) explores the different ways groups remember the historical experiences of their societies, particularly traumatic experiences like war, famine, genocide, and terrorism. In survivors of the First World War and the Vietnam War, for example, Edkins finds a distinction between personal memories and the "act of remembering." The former, memory, is a personal record of direct experience. The latter is a "social" experience that is "intensely political" (Edkins 2003, 54). Likewise, Dyson and Preston (2006) find that individuals consistently express themselves with analogies not from past personal events, but from past events with broad societal significance. For example, the idea that the United States is exceptional, a "shining city upon a hill," is based on that state's unique political history. Many Americans *feel* that because their history is "exceptional", the United States has special rights, responsibilities, and obligations toward others (McCormick 1992: 8).

The "social" act of remembering is "political" because it triggers a collective response from the nation, building an emotional bond between members. Indeed, collective emotions and the formation and preservation of national identity are closely related. Gellner (1983: 37) and Guibernau (2004: 136) argue that to identify with a specific nation, an individual must develop "a strong emotional investment" because national identity "arises from the consciousness of forming a group based on the 'felt' closeness uniting those who belong to the nation." More recent studies point to the interrelated, even co-constitutive, relationship between collective emotion and identity, arguing that "emotion makes identity consequential, and identity makes group-level emotion possible" (Mercer 2014: 522). Hagström and Gustafsson (2015: 10) note that national identity is "constructed through the forging of an emotional allegiance that makes us feel like we belong. ... Without emotional attachment, identities are difficult to construct." In short, shared historical experiences are what generate "collective affective experiences" (Hall and Ross 2015: 859) and thus what build the bonds of national solidarity (Hutchison 2010). This finding, again, supports the idea that historical experiences, especially such traumatic experiences as war, genocide, terrorism, or colonialism, establish social coherence within the nation and sharpen the distinction between "us" and "them."

South Korean national identity: Formation and evolution

The conceptual review above helps us understand that national identity may work as a causal influence on a state's external behaviour. The following case study of South Korea illustrates how national identity actually plays a causal role in foreign policy actions. It begins with an excavation, if you will, of South Korean national identity and ends with an examination of specific foreign policies that are either constrained or promoted by the South Korean national identity.

In the nineteenth century, national identity unified decentralised ethnic groups in places like Germany and Italy into distinct political and territorial states. In Europe, national identity was a way of unifying ethnic groups and drawing borders between them. In Korea, scholars also refer to a "collective notion of national identity" (Choe 2006: 93) based on a belief in "ethnic homogeneity" and a "prehistoric origin" (Shin and Chang 2004: 119–124). This is a textbook definition of ethnically centred national identity that could, just as correctly, apply to European nationalism. Unlike in Europe, however, a millennium of political, linguistic, and geographic "continuity" left little need for ethnic unification in nineteenth-century Korea (Shin and Chang 2004: 121). The gravest threat to Korean national integrity in the nineteenth century was Western imperialism. To confront imperialist power, Korean nationalists felt a strong need to assert the distinctiveness and effectiveness of their nation and thus mitigate foreign influence and aggression. Politicians used Korean national identity, then, mainly as "an anti-imperialist ideology, opposing foreign challenge or aggression" (Shin, Freda, and Yi 1999: 470; Olsen 2008).

When, in the early twentieth century, Korea entered the international order as a modern nation-state, a national identity based on ethnicity prevailed. The Japanese annexation of Korea from 1910 until 1943 only strengthened the idea of a distinct ethnically Korean national identity. A state-centred national identity based on statehood alone – if it had ever existed[1] – completely lost its basis among the Korean people when they lost their sovereignty. Without a state, Koreans relied on "ethnic homogeneity" and common ancestry to maintain a national identity that drew a sharp distinction between themselves and the Japanese aggressor. Against this backdrop, Koreans stopped using the word "*gukmin*," which means "citizen of the state," and instead used "*minjok*," which means "a common ethnic group" (Choe 2006: 95). The Korean nation was "racialized through belief in a common pre-historic origin, responding to Western imperialism, especially Japanese imperialism" (Shin et al. 1999: 469). Under colonialism, ethnicity or "race" served as a powerful differentiator and solidifier for Koreans.

Specific colonial policies, such as forced assimilation, encouraged the growth of ethnically centred nationalist sentiment in Korea, including the growth of an understanding of nation and identity that were insepar-able from race. The Japanese adopted aggressive policies to assimilate Koreans into Imperial Japan and used the argument of Japanese racial and cultural superiority to justify their annexation of Korea. In response, Korean thought began to privilege the distinctiveness, purity, and superiority of the *Korean* ethnicity (Allen 1990; Koh 1994; Shin et al. 1999). Koreans, in particular teachers and journalists, zealously advo-cated for Korean "ethnic nationalism." To rationalise their beliefs, they built narratives around common ancestry, "ethnic homogeneity," and a long and glorious Korean history (Allen 1990: 792). While ethnicity (a cultural construct based on common ancestry, language, and his-tory) is typically distinct from race (an immutable phenotypic and genotypic group), Koreans viewed the two as inseparable. In Korean discourse about identity, for example, the terms "race," "ethnicity," and "nation" are used interchangeably (Shin and Chang 2004: 121). During this period, the notion of "a nation of one clan" (or "*danil minjok*" in Korean) came to occupy a hegemonic position in the Korean discourse on national identity. Korean identity became all but inseparable from ethnicity and race.

Another traumatic historical experience, the Korean War of 1950 to 1953, added a second layer of complexity to Korean national identity that was not at all congruent with the notion of "ethnic homogeneity."

During the war, the South and North adopted political identities that were not only distinct from but also in stark opposition to each other. In South Korea, for example, politicians portrayed the communist political system in Pyongyang as threatening and antagonistic (Bleiker 2001: 121; Shin et al. 1999: 472; Olsen 2008: 10). The Korean War brought about a fundamental change in the structure of South Korea's national identity. After the war, South Koreans internalised liberal market values and democracy as another way to identify the "self" against the "other" in the North. These post-war values were, and are, somewhat at odds with the primary sources of Korean national identity: ethnicity and race.

Despite the territorial division, ethnicity remains today a reminder in both South and North Korea of "who they are." Neither territorial partition nor political separation completely erased the belief in a Korean identity based on a shared past, common ancestry, and ethnic homogeneity. The view that all Koreans are "members of an extended family" is a resilient one. In explaining this phenomenon, Choe (2006) notes that the territorial division of Korea was initially *externally* driven by the Cold War system. The governments of both South and North Korea continue to regard the reunification of Korea as the key to the "completion" of the nation-state. Both consider the division of Korea after the Second World War a "temporary" circumstance (Shin et al. 1999: 476). The leitmotif of ethnically based national identity is a critical component of policy discourses on the reunification of Korea.

After the territorial division, the more or less unitary system of ethnic national identity in South Korea gave way to an identity affected by multiple variables with asymmetrical degrees of rigidity. Nonetheless, ethnic identity remains the most fundamental and rigid of these variables. In South Korea, the powerful idea of a mythic historical Korean nation persists. A unique racial and ethnic heritage is believed to be the thing that most clearly distinguishes this nation from others, particularly Japan. Whether true or constructed, this difference binds South and North Koreans together despite their contrasting political regimes. Political ideology is another identity influencer, however. Political identity operates on a less rigid and more contextual level, but there are political (democratic) and economic (open market) aspects to South Korean identity. Because the values of democracy and market capitalism are not uniquely Korean, they are less "essential" than ethnicity and therefore more fluid. Indeed, as codified in historical myth, the nation-state of Korea existed for a millennium without these political values.

South Korea's layered national identity means that its people have a complex, even contradictory perception of their neighbour to the north. South Koreans who fully embrace their ethnic identity often empathise with North Korea, or at least its people. South Koreans who identify strongly with the political identity of the nation, in contrast, are very critical of North Korea, or at least its regime in Pyongyang. They oppose, for example, sending economic aid from South to North Korea, lest that aid bolster the communist regime. Still, operating within the belief of a common Korean ethnic identity, even many critical South Koreans believe that it is their state's "duty" to liberate their "brothers and sisters" in the North from the communist regime (Koh 1994; Choe 2006). Although wary of potential military provocations from Pyongyang, those critical of the communist regime maintain that disputes between North and South Korea are "internal" matters of one people, rather than "international" disputes (Lee and Jeong 2010; Kim 2011).

In contrast, South Koreans have a set perception of Japan as the immutable "other." Most Koreans support the notion that all Koreans are ethnically similar and members of an extended family. In post-colonial Korean society, however, Japan is still a powerful differentiator that reminds Koreans of who they are and who they are not. Since the colonial occupation of the early twentieth century, the idea of the Japanese "other," a foil to Korean ethnicity, has built bonds of national solidary and social coherence among South Koreans. South Korean sentiment and, to an extent, even its history curricula support the idea that the Korean nation is not only distinct from Japan, but ethnically superior as well. The image of Japan in South Korea, then, is somewhat more consistent – and more consistently negative – than the image of North Korea.

South Korean foreign policy actions towards North Korea and Japan

The multifaceted ethnic and political identity of South Korea is reflected in the state's foreign policies towards North Korea and Japan. South Korea's conflicting perception of North Korea – as both an ethnic identical and a communist "other" – have led to somewhat contradictory policies towards the state. In contrast, South Korea maintains a deter-minedly cold relationship with its former coloniser, Japan, even though the two countries are thriving democracies with close economic ties.

Since the end of the Korean War in 1953, South Korean governments have debated which foreign policy strategy the state should adopt with regard to North Korea. Generally speaking, the government has been split between those preferring containment and strict reciprocity and those endorsing sympathetic engagement and dialogue. The administrations of Kim Dae-jung (1998–2003) and Roh Moo-hyun (2003–2008), for example, pursued dialogue, engagement, and reconciliation – the so-called "Sunshine Policy" – towards North Korea. South Korea kept up its Sunshine Policy even when Pyongyang revealed its ambitions to develop nuclear weapons, withdrew from the Nuclear Non-Proliferation Treaty, and, in effect, destabilised Asian regional security. The Kim and Roh administrations continued to send North Korea economic aid and engage in military dialogues with the state. In this respect, analysts have portrayed the Sunshine Policy as "underbalancing" (Kim 2011). From a realist security theory perspective, the Sunshine Policy is puzzling. Yet, when one takes into account the in-group bias of South Korean policymakers towards a racial and ethnic Korean nation, the policy is more logical, or at least more understandable. In the discourse around the Sunshine Policy, the governments often evoked the Korean term *"danil minjok"* or *"han minjok,"* which literally means "a nation of one clan" (Roh 2006a). Despite North Korea's military adventurism, South Korea pursued cooperative and sympathetic policies towards the neighbouring state based on, or caused by, a rigid sense of shared ethnic identity.

The foreign policy of the Lee Myung-bak government (2008–2012) is perhaps a richer example of how national identity causes a state's specific policies. Unlike his two predecessors, Lee took a hard-line approach to the regime in Pyongyang. He justified this approach by pointing to the increasingly bellicose actions of North Korea (at the time, the state was conducting nuclear weapons tests and long-range missile launches). Lee evoked the political, state-centred identity of South Korea to drum up opposition to these actions. The administration often described the regime in Pyongyang as brutal and irrational and drew a stark distinction between it and the morally superior and economically advanced system in South Korea. The Lee administration called its hard-line strategy a "grand bargain" aimed at pushing the North Korean political and economic system towards democracy and liberalism. South Korea, positioning itself as the more advanced state, differentiated and infantilised the communist political identity of North Korea. The state abandoned sympathetic aid and adopted a policy of strict reciprocity towards North Korea in the realm of trade (Klinger 2008).

As had been the case with previous administrations, however, the Lee administration also considered the peaceful reunification of Korea a national goal. Policymakers still frequently used the term *"danil minjok"* in their policy discourses on North Korea (Lee 2010a, 2010b,

2012) and, even as Pyongyang continued to militarise, South Korea consistently pursued peaceful reunification. In 2010, for example, the South Korean battleship *Cheonan* sank in the Yellow Sea, killing 46 South Koreans. All evidence pointed to North Korea being behind the attack, but despite it being a clear violation of international law and a justification for a declaration of war, the Lee administration did not pursue a military response. Instead, it imposed economic sanctions against Pyongyang. Although Lee officially blamed North Korea for sinking the *Cheonan*, he also stated that the North "must stop committing reckless military provocations, and embark on the path toward common prosperity for all 70 million Koreans. By doing so, we must restore peace and stability on the Korean peninsula and find the road to common prosperity for the Korean people. *Our ultimate goal is not military confrontation but peaceful unification*" (Lee 2010a, emphasis added).

Lee's statement reveals that, despite his emphasis on a South Korean political identity distinct from that of the North, ethnic (*minjok*) identity was also a *constraining* influence on the foreign policy of his administration. For much of his career, Lee spoke of South Korean identity as inseparable from democracy and the market economy. Even so, a deep ethnic identity shared across North and South restricted the range of "acceptable" policies towards North Korea. After the *Cheonan* went down, policymakers did not put forward resolutions to sever all relations with the North, let alone declare war (Lee 2013). Several public opinion polls taken *after* the *Cheonan* incident indicated that 55.2 per cent of South Koreans favoured "reconciliation and cooperation" while significantly fewer, 42.7 per cent, favoured taking a hard-line stance against the North (Lee and Jeong 2010). It is clear that while the Lee government took a harder stance against North Korea than its predecessors, a feeling of residual ethnic solidarity with the North limited the range of acceptable foreign policy actions to, mostly, those that promoted "reconciliation and cooperation." These empirical findings show that socially constructed national identity works as a constraining and enabling cause in foreign policy. Furthermore, the extent of national identity's causal influence varies depending on the type of national identity – political or ethnic, for example – and how rigid it is.

While South Korea's foreign policy towards North Korea varies based on ethnic and political identity, all South Korean governments, regardless of their political ideologies, have taken an almost unitarily vigilant course of action towards Japan. Although South Korean presidents emphasise, rhetorically, the need for reconciliation and cooperation with Japan when they come into office, most of their foreign policies in office are not consistent with this rhetoric. Both the left-wing administrations of Kim Dae-jung and Roh Moo-hyun and the right-wing Lee Myung-bak administration emphasised a "future-oriented relationship" between Seoul and Tokyo based on "a spirit of reconciliation and friendship." Yet, all three administrations were bogged down in disputes with Japan. South Korea took offense, for example, to Japanese history textbooks that whitewash the state's colonial wrongdoings. The two states also butt heads over the islands known as Dokdo in South Korea and as Takeshima in Japan. The islands were annexed by Japan in 1905 ahead of its colonisation of the Korean peninsula and are currently under South Korean jurisdiction.

These disputes with Japan elicit a "collective emotional" response – mostly anger and fear – from South Koreans. In such an environment, achieving inter-state cooperation, let alone political friendship, is a tall order. In disputes with Japan, South Korean presidents take a – sometimes disproportionately – hard-line stance against Japan, making comments like: "they [the Japanese] need to face the truth about their past, reflect on it and make a genuine apology" (Roh 2006a). For Koreans, the territorial dispute over the Dokdo islands is also a dispute over the history, dignity, and sovereignty of Korea (Roh 2006b; Lee 2013). The reasoning behind this belief was revealed in the statement made by the former South Korean foreign minister Kim Sung-hwan to the Associated Press: "We are victims of Japanese colonial rule. ... When the Japanese government claims that Dokdo is their territory, Korean people see it as another attempt to invade our country" (Kim 2012). Indeed, in a 2014 survey, South Koreans saw Japan as their second-largest military threat (EAI 2014: 24). Even though North Korea is objectively the bigger threat, South Korea and Japan have trouble cooperating. The Lee administration, for example, refused to sign the General Security of Military Information Agreement, an intelligence-sharing pact with Japan that would have consolidated information on North Korea's military and nuclear threats. Many South Koreans opposed the agreement, insisting that, before they began cooperating with the Japanese, Tokyo should offer a sincere apology for colonialism.

South Korea often eyes Japan's ambitions in East Asia with suspicion. To some, any attempt by Japan to reclaim the role of regional hegemon brings back the ghosts of imperialism. To many Koreans, instead of taking on regional leadership, Japan should be atoning quietly for its colonialist past. The collective memory of colonialism – part of the Korean identity – continues to cause conflict between South Korea and Japan on the international stage. The ethnicity-centred Korean identity defines the view of Japan that South Koreans, including decision-makers, use to interpret Japanese policies. Suspicion about Japan's regional intentions reproduces and reinforces the image of Japan as a coloniser. Ethnicity-centred identity also provides normative guidelines for South Korea's overarching approach to foreign policy with Japan that endure from administration to administration.

Implications for "global IR" and dialogue

The above empirical analysis and its findings have significant implications for the ongoing project to broaden IR and our calls for dialogue in the discipline. The findings show that without local context, mainstream (Western-centric) realist and liberal IR theories are unable to offer a satisfactory answer to why South Korea behaved as it did in relation to North Korea or Japan. Indigenous knowledge can also add depth and sophistication to constructivist IR theory by specifying its boundary and scope conditions. Knowledge about local historical experiences, for example, makes constructivism a more effective approach to understanding the dynamics and extent of national identity's causal effect on foreign policy. Such knowledge is indeed necessary to determine which aspects of national identity are more rigid and thus exercise a more powerful causal influence on foreign policy, and to understand why. In short, this indigenous knowledge helps increase the analytical purchase of national identity, a key variable of constructivism. Let me clarify these points further.

First, the empirical findings demonstrate that South Korea has a multilevel structure of national identity in which different types of identity operate with *asymmetric* rigidity. The findings also show that the different types of national identity have constrained or facilitated South Korea's foreign policy actions, defying the conventional expectations of mainstream IR (i.e. realist and liberal) theories. Regarding North Korea's nuclear weapons and Japan's history textbooks, for example, South Korea reacted more firmly and even aggressively in the case of the latter, even though the issue is not an immediate threat to Seoul's survival. In other words, the pattern of South Korean behaviour towards North Korea and Japan might be seen as irrational from the perspective of realist and liberal IR theories. Consider, for example, the present security environment of East Asia. South Korea directly faces North Korea's nuclear threats; in order to curtail the latter's nuclear ambitions, South Korea is in serious need of cooperation and coordination with regional states, including Japan. Seoul also needs to consider the trilateral cooperation system of the United States-Japan-South Korea, which the United States, in the context of dealing with the rise of China, has pressured it to join. On top of these issues, both South

Korea and Japan are democracies with thick economic ties; several economic and cultural institutions have been established to promote the bilateral cooperation between the two countries. As such, realist and liberal theory – specifically balance of power theory, balance of threat theory, neo-liberal institutionalism, economic liberalism, and democratic peace theory – would all expect South Korea to pursue comprehensive cooperation with Japan. In short, given both external (geopolitical) conditions and domestic political and economic systems, one would expect South Korean behaviour towards Japan and North Korea to be an easy case that confirms the theoretical expectations of realism and liberalism. Nevertheless, the empirical findings show the opposite.

Although South Korean foreign policy behaviour does not follow the theoretical propositions of realism and liberalism, it appears to confirm the utility of constructivism, which holds that what matters in international politics is socially constructed ideas. That is, South Korean behaviour becomes understandable when we consider South Korea's long-standing ethnic identity, according to which Japan is regarded as an *inferior other*. Of course, this conclusion does not simply reveal the victory of constructivist IR theory over its realist and liberal counterparts. More careful and sophisticated thinking is necessary here. As the above empirical findings indicate, a state's national identity can consist of more than one element, not all of which have the same causal import. In the case of South Korea, it is its ethnic identity that acts as a rigid constraining and enabling cause. The socio-historically and socio-emotionally entrenched notion of ethnic homogeneity has played a key role in defining who Koreans are, and it has affected South Korean foreign policy as a perceptual filter and cognitive constraint, shaping policymakers' normative and practical horizons. From this finding, important insights into theoretical dialogue can be drawn.

As the existing constructivist literature indicates, national identity matters. But how it matters and the extent to which it matters depend on the types of national identity involved and their degree of rigidity, and rigidity is dependent on collective memories and emotions regarding certain historical experiences. More specifically, national identity has a substantial causal influence on the process of making foreign policy. It shapes policymakers' behavioural motivations, frames the normative context in which policymakers perceive and act in their world, and rationalises specific, as well as overarching, foreign policy decisions. In short, national identity can be a constraining and enabling cause in the making of foreign policy. Moreover, multiple national identities can be preserved in a state over time; among them, a particular one will be more rigid or fundamental than the others; its causal power (i.e. its constraining and enabling influence) over a state's foreign policy over-whelms other types of national identity. Hence, in order to increase the explanatory purchase of national identity, analysts need to understand not just any national identity of a given state, but the one that is rigid. This is where IR theories, specifically constructivist theorists, should be attentive to local, indigenous knowledge, precisely because the national identity that is rigid is the one that has been stable over time, is shared across generations, and continues to engender emotional bonds in a given nation. In addition, as the investigation of how South Korean national identity was formed demonstrates, the substantive elements of the rigid national identity are derived from the nation's collective historical experiences, especially its traumatic experiences – such as colonialism or war – in which the distinction between *self* and *other* (or *us* and *them*) is clear and consistent and, thus, underlies and ensures the social coherence and emotional solidarity of the nation. This, once again, asks IR theory to be attentive to the history or experiences of the nation under study. In sum, we should not only examine the various aspects of a state's identity, but also evaluate the rigidity of these aspects to correctly understand their effect. To this end, Western-centric IR theory, including con-structivism, needs indigenous knowledge (of Asia) and vice versa. Indeed, these can and should be interweaved.

As many scholars have recently argued, looking at the world from a perspective that privileges Western veins of thought leaves much open to misinterpretation. But the opposite is also true. The recent calls for a more inclusive and broader IR – "post-Western" or "Global" IR – that properly reflects the histories, knowledge, and theoretical perspectives outside of the West do "not seek to displace existing (or future) theories of IR that may substantially originate from Western ideas and experi-ences" (Acharya 2014: 649). Instead, the ultimate objective of these attempts to broaden IR is to recognise multiple foundations of thought and encourage dialogue across the theoretical and spatial divides in the study of global politics.

If so, debates over Western versus non-Western IR or the superiority of one theoretical approach over another should not be a major issue of concern. Instead, the question should be when and where each approach offers greater insights and, most importantly, how fruitful interaction between them can be encouraged. As Table 5.1 shows, by spelling out the theoretical meanings of the local experiences of Asia in relation to IR theory's causal mechanisms or boundary conditions, we can establish and expand useful points of contact across disciplinary divides and thus promote dialogue that avoids a narcissistic turf war. Rather than unquestioningly applying or utterly rejecting existing

Table 5.1 An example: Dialogue between Western-centric IR theory (i.e. constructivism) and indigenous knowledge and experiences in East Asia

	Western IR theory	Dialogue — Indigenous, empirical knowledge of Asia
General propositions induced from constructivism	National identity matters in international politics	**Testing proposition:** Yes
Remaining puzzles	*How* does it matter?	**Enriching proposition:** • National identity acts as a prism through which policymakers interpret situations to be compatible with prevailing societal norms • National identity contains normative regularities that make policymakers self-regulate their actions • Foreign policy may be based on certain national goals that are part of the national identity
	When does it matter most?	**Specifying scope conditions:** • When a particular identity that indicates the clear distinction between "self" and "other" is invoked • When a particular identity that forges national solidarity and emotional bonds is invoked • Such identity is based on a nation's collective experiences, especially traumatic historical experiences
Benefits of having dialogue in the way suggested here		• Greater richness in understanding and higher precision in explanation • Better suggestions for real-world problems and policy issues

(Western-centric) IR theories, our aim should be to interweave these theories with indigenous experiences in the non-West and thereby refine and remould the theories or create inclusive and complementary models of our complex world. After all, the issue is not who or what is right or wrong, but *whether we can talk to each other.*

Note

1 Some scholars argue that there was little, if any, "feeling of loyalty" towards the abstract concept of Korea as "a nation-state" prior to the late nineteenth century (Eckert 1991: 226).

6 Conclusion
Reflexive solidarity

Tim Dunne, Milja Kurki, and Steve Smith (2013b: 7) write that "the field is now much healthier because of the proliferation of theories." Similarly, Nicholas Rengger (2015: 32) notes that IR is "a plural ... field. Whether one likes it or not, ... that is simply the reality." Of course, their observations are correct – in a certain sense. IR has a more varied theoretical palette today than it did in the 1980s. Yet this is true mainly in terms of the number of theories that exist in the field. Diversity and pluralism in IR, however, should not only involve theory as such, but also epistemology and methodology that underlie the building and operation of theory. If we assess "the proliferation of theories" in IR on this basis, our assessment of whether IR truly is a "plural" field and "much healthier" is likely to differ. Indeed, as the investigations in Chapters 2, 3, and 5 show, extant concerns about the parochialism of IR are legitimate. Geo-culturally, non-Western voices and experiences have yet to be reflected in the overall theoretical terrain of contemporary IR. As well, an epistemological and methodological monoculture centred on positivism prevails across geo-cultural borders. Although there are various (Western) post-positivist theories, they have failed to transform disciplinary practices, and especially educational practices. Furthermore, the marginalisation of post-positivist scholarship in IR exists everywhere, the West and the non-West alike. In short, when diversity is understood in this more nuanced way, IR does not appear to be especially diverse. This situation is puzzling given that there have been constant calls for more diversity in IR theory and greater pluralism in the field. As David Lake has recently argued, "promoting diversity in universities and societies ... is an important goal *in itself*," and we can be "better scholars" by "promoting diversity in the academy" (2016: 1112, exmphasis added).

A crucial question, then, is: how can we open up IR?

Reflexive solidarity

This question was addressed in Chapter 4 in the context of disciplinary socialisation. In that chapter, I discussed how IR is researched, published, and taught, and I referred to the importance of "reflexive solidarity," an encounter between self-reflexivity and collective solidarity. Let me clarify this further.

First, if we aim to open up IR, especially in praxical and geo-cultural terms, we must ensure that IR is researched and taught in a way that more fully endorses the validity of a wide range of epistemological, theoretical, methodological, and empirical/spatial perspectives. IR publication systems and pedagogy are socially and normatively constructed and thus play a direct role in selecting and eliminating practices closely related to the reproduction of the hierarchical order of knowledge in the discipline. The existing mainstream (i.e. Western/positivist) views are reproduced through these mechanisms, as a result of which the intellectual "monoculture" remains unchanged. It is here that our calls for diversity and pluralism must be linked to reflexivity, the first element of "reflexive solidarity."

Reflexivity: Two interwoven roles

Reflexivity plays two interwoven roles. First, it asks us to keep reminding ourselves that the present structure of IR is *of our own making* and that key agents in this making are individual scholars. This realisation makes it easier for us to recognise and explore previously under-recognised causes of the dominance of the field by one particular way of thinking (e.g. not only socio-epistemic causes, but also, and more importantly, individual-praxical ones). Once scholars recognise this, they are more ready to acknowledge the following: if we are still living in a "Western/positivist-centric" IR world, the world has emerged out of our own practice – as individuals and as a collective – and willingness to persist with the mainstream perspective as a result of social and institutional incentives and disincentives. If not from us, then from where? *Ex nihilo*? IR as an academic discipline is what we make of it. A meaningful change in the discipline – that is, moving IR toward a more diverse and pluralistic field of study, especially in terms of practice and geo-cultures – requires a robust recognition of this point.

This leads to the second role of reflexivity: critical self-reflection. More concretely, recognising that the structure of the disciplinary system of IR is of our own making can lead us to realise that it is we scholars who have the ability to change the field; this in turn opens up the possibility for self-reflection and self-awareness in regard to the following questions: What do we research philosophically, theoretically, methodologically, geopolitically, or empirically? How do we carry out peer review of other research? And most importantly, what and how do we teach in the classroom? In other words, we are led to critically ask ourselves whether our research and teaching practices have been rich enough to go beyond mainstream IR and do justice to pluralism in both our publications and our classrooms. If our calls for a pluralistic and inclusive IR fail to generate a substantive set of practices, this is because we do not properly practice what we preach.

Such critical self-reflection provides the necessary motivation to bring about greater diversity in IR theory and practice. With regard to a "stronger" reflexivity in IR (see, e.g., Guzzini 2013; Sylvester 2013; Tickner 2013; Hamati-Ataya 2014), our focus should be on not only IR (meta)theory, but also individual theorists. Recall that the once-dominant positivism has met its demise in the philosophy of science and that, within the philosophy of science, it is indeed "critically reflexive" scholars such as Kuhn, Lakatos, Feyerabend, and (the later) Wittgenstein who have played a crucial role in this demise. Without critical *self*-reflection, the "performativity" with which our calls for pluralism should be accompanied is likely to remain truncated. The practice of pluralism, after all, begins with the self. Only when critical self-reflection functions as a leitmotif for pluralism in IR will socialised disciplinary mechanisms, such as the Western/positivist-centred IR publication system and pedagogy, be changed in ways that not only accept a flourishing of diverse experiences, theories, and methodologies, but also convey that flourishing in texts and classrooms.

Surely, as Dunne, Hansen, and Wight comment, "structurally, there are strong incentives" to reproduce or support dominant theory (Dunne et al. 2013a: 417).[1] To put it differently, there are disincentives to fail to conform to IR's dominant/mainstream views and practices. In the name of a standard or "scientific" approach, mainstream IR theory or methodology exerts a substantial influence on our behaviour, affecting opportunities for publication, research grants, and academic positions, all of which are critical to our standing as both academics and individuals. Given this structural constraint of the discipline, it may sound like wishful thinking to anticipate that critical self-reflexivity can change the current state of IR.

At the same time, however, IR is also a world in which scholars are the most powerful agents in shaping the world. As peer reviewers, editors, examiners, chairs, supervisors, and teachers, individual scholars can bring change and diversity to the field. Again, our behaviour is constrained by structural conditions, such as disciplinary norms that reflect the dominant view. But this does not mean that we are powerless. Compared with other types of social actors, scholars are relatively free agents. The structure of IR is largely derived from our disciplinary socialisation practices. Indeed, all social structures are, in Max Weber's (1968: 13) words, "the resultants and modes of organizations of the specific acts of individual men." To be sure, once established, those structures exhibit a certain uniqueness of ontological characteristics, which in turn constrains "the acts of individual men." But whatever the structural constraints, what is presented to us – for example, a lack of epistemological or geographical diversity in IR – has not been determined by the structural conditions as such. Ontologically speaking, it is human agents' intentions and actions that give rise to such structural conditions. We do have a capacity to consciously act and, in doing so, realise our intentions. This is especially so within academia, where scholars have a significant degree of agency, free will, and creativity.

In this vein, we scholars are what Antonio Gramsci (1971) calls "organic intellectuals." We are not merely consumers and producers of ideas and ideologies, but "organic organisers" of them and thus, in Gramscian terms, "organisers of hegemony." We, as organic intellectuals, play a central role in formulating "common sense" – although that common sense should be criticised, according to Gramsci, for leading the masses to believe in ahistorical and "extra-human" realities and "naïve metaphysics" (Gramsci 1971: 199, 441). Further, organic intellectuals have the capability to politically organise the masses by exercising "intellectual and moral leadership" (Gramsci 1971: 57) and as such can provide "cohesion and guidance to hegemony" (Zahran and Ramos 2011: 28). By the same token, however, if we are in the position to offer "cohesion and guidance" in regard to (political or epistemic) hegemony, we can also weaken that hegemony by exercising the same "intellectual and moral leadership" in a way that repudiates or transcends the dominant way of governing or knowing.

Encounters between self-reflexivity and collective solidarity

This is, I believe, where advocates of broadening IR, especially those engaged in the "non-Western" IR theorisation project, ought to reconsider their narrowly conceived approaches to the project and instead seek alliances with others whose voices remain at the margins of the field. Although we, as organic intellectuals, can deliver "intellectual and moral leadership" in ways that help increase diversity in IR and unsettle the mainstream paradigm, it is unlikely that a push for reform will come from within the mainstream IR paradigm. John Mearsheimer (2016: 147), a mainstream IR theorist, has explicitly distanced himself from recent calls to broaden the theoretical horizons of IR beyond Western/American dominance. As David Lake argues in his paper "White Man's IR: An Intellectual Confession," attempts to enhance diversity are "often resented by currently privileged groups … as a 'watering down' of standards in the discipline" (Lake 2016: 1117). The mainstream of the profession creates "a self-reinforcing community standard" by acting as "gatekeepers" regarding what gets studied and how. Although "privileged" groups in IR – for example, white men working in the American academy – are "rarely self-conscious in their biases and even less … intentional in their exclusionary practices" (Lake 2016: 1116), their practice tends to conform to *the discipline of the discipline*. Who, then, is likely to exercise the intellectual and moral leadership necessary to unsettle the discipline? Marginalised scholars. Since their views, their experiences, and their scholarship are marginalised, they are more likely to attempt to change the parochial landscape of IR or break the disciplinary hierarchy. Indeed, they should do so if their calls to broaden IR are to be realised.

Furthermore, since their voices remain marginal, they need allies – not only to have their voices heard but, more importantly, to have them accepted as legitimate. Given their marginalised position in the field, their critical self-reflection needs to be performed in association with collective solidarity. Only then can their potential "intellectual and moral leadership" lead to meaningful results.

To this end, what the "non-Western" IR theorisation enterprise should do first is widen the discussion by considering the issue of marginalisation beyond geographical concerns. As noted, "the current West-centrism of IR" (Buzan 2016: 156), is not only a geographical issue but also an epistemological and methodological one. The hierarchy of knowledge and scholarship cuts across several realms of inquiry in IR. In particular, the lack of diversity in the field extends to issues of epistemology and methodology. Specific methodological precepts that flow from positivist epistemology, such as operationalisation, quantification, and generalisation, prevail over the entire discipline of political science, including IR, *across* different (whether Western or non-Western) IR communities. As such, marginalisation is a powerful issue that can find resonance in both non-Western and post-positivist IR scholarships. This is why I have proposed "reflexive solidarity," an encounter between self-reflexivity and collective solidarity. This is also why advocates of "non-Western" IR theorisation need to revamp their geography-orientated ways of addressing the complex problematic of marginalisation and instead seek solidarity with others whose voices also remain at the margins of the field. Because the current parochialism of IR is not only geopolitical but also epistemological and methodological, the ongoing projects of "non-Western" IR theory building need to refocus their attention, broadening the range of their own questions and undertakings.

The "non-Western" IR theory-building enterprise is based on the view that where a theory originates and who originates it matter a great deal. This belief resonates with post-positivist understandings of theory. In contrast to positivist epistemology, in which theory is thought to be objective and neutral – regardless of where and by whom a theory is built – post-positivism emphasises that "theory is always *for* someone and *for* some purpose" (Cox 1981: 128, emphasis in original). In this regard, post-positivist scholarship engages in critical, normative, and constitutive theorising, as opposed to explanatory theorising. Post-positivist epistemology regards the key roles of theory as criticising a particular social order and analysing how it is constituted, with the goal of changing it. "Non-Western" IR projects also want to change IR, to make it more colourful, especially in a geo-cultural sense. In short, an encounter between non-Western and post-positivist scholarship is not just possible, but also necessary if we are to achieve a more diverse and pluralistic IR.

Whether to welcome and practice diverse epistemologies, theories, methodologies, histories, and experiences that do not depend on the dominant paradigm in IR is an issue that can be decided by the key agents in the discipline, namely IR scholars. Yet this by no means indicates that any or every individual scholar will attempt to open up the field. Indeed, attempts to unsettle the present hierarchical structure of the discipline face constraints. The role of denaturalising main-stream norms and practices falls to critical, conscious, and reflexive individual agents. In order for their agential power and leadership to be more fully harnessed in the opening up of IR, critical self-reflection and collective empathy and collaboration among marginalised scholars are all essential. By bringing this reflexive solidary to our everyday debate on "non-Western" IR, new and diverse ways of "doing" IR and thus "knowing" international relations can flourish.

Note

1 In their study, two important questions remain under-illuminated. First, how is the standard approach to IR reproduced? Arlene Tickner (2013: 628) has recently observed that "many aspects of the inner workings of IR

continue to be underexplored." The second, and in my view more important, question is: what is required if IR scholars are to preserve their maximum autonomy within the disciplinary mechanisms and processes, or to change those mechanisms and processes? This latter question is closely related to the "reflexive solidarity" advocated here.

References

Acharya, Amitav (2014) Global International Relations (IR) and Regional Worlds: A New Agenda for International Studies. *International Studies Quarterly* 58(4): 647–659.

Acharya, Amitav (2016) Advancing Global IR: Challenges, Contentions, and Contributions. *International Studies Review* 18(1): 4–15.

Acharya, Amitav and Barry Buzan (eds) (2010) *Non-Western International Relations Theory: Perspectives on and Beyond Asia.* London and New York: Routledge.

Ackerly, Brooke and Jacqui True (2008) Reflexivity in Practice: Power and Ethics in Feminist Research on International Relations. *International Studies Review* 10(4): 693–707.

Ackerly, Brooke, Maria Stern, and Jacqui True (eds) (2006) *Feminist Methodologies for International Relations.* Cambridge: Cambridge University Press.

Alker, Hayward (1996) *Rediscoveries and Reformulations: Humanistic Methodologies for International Studies.* Cambridge: Cambridge University Press.

Allen, Chizuko (1990) Northeast Asia Centered around Korea: Choi Namsun's View of History. *Journal of Asian Studies* 49(4): 787–806.

Aradau, Claudia and Jef Huysmans (2014) Critical Methods in International Relations: The Politics of Tools, Devices and Acts. *European Journal of International Relations* 20(3): 596–619.

Arai, Tatsushi, Shihoko Goto, and Zheng Wang (eds) (2013) *Clash of National Identities: China, Japan and the China Sea Territorial Dispute.* Washington, DC: Wilson Center.

Archer, Margaret, Roy Bhaskar, Andrew Collier, Tony Lawson, and Alan Norrie (eds) (1998) *Critical Realism: Essential Readings.* London and New York: Routledge.

Ashley, Richard K. (1984) The Poverty of Neorealism. *International Organization* 38(2): 225–286.

Ashley, Richard K. and R. B. J. Walker (1990) Speaking the Language of Exile: Dissident Thought in International Studies. *International Studies Quarterly* 34(3): 259–268.

Barkin, J. Samuel and Laura Sjoberg (2015a) Calculating Critique: Thinking Outside the Methods Matching Game. *Millennium: Journal of International Studies* 43(3): 852–871.

Barkin, J. Samuel and Laura Sjoberg (2015b) Why Quantitative Methods for Critical Theorizing? In Samuel Barkin and Laura Sjoberg (eds) *Quantitative Methods for Critical and Constructivist International Relations*. Ann Arbor, MI: University of Michigan Press, 1–24.

Barkin, J. Samuel and Laura Sjoberg (eds) (2017) *Interpretive Quantification: Methodological Explorations for Critical and Constructivist IR*. Ann Arbor, MI: University of Michigan Press.

Bell, Duncan (2003) Mythscapes: Memory, Mythology, and National Identity. *British Journal of Sociology* 54(1): 63–81.

Bennett, Andrew (2015) Found in Translation: Combining Discourse Analysis with Computer Assisted Content Analysis. *Millennium: Journal of International Studies* 43(3): 984–997.

Bhaskar, Roy (1978) *A Realist Theory of Science*. Brighton: Harvester Press.

Bhaskar, Roy (1982) Emergence, Explanation and Emancipation. In Paul F. Secord (ed.) *Explaining Human Behavior: Consciousness, Human Action and Social Structure*. Beverly Hills: Sage Publications, 275–310.

Biersteker, Thomas J. (2009) The Parochialism of Hegemony: Challenges for "American" International Relations. In Arlene B. Tickner and Ole Wæver (eds) *International Relations Scholarship Around the World*. London: Routledge, 308–327.

Bilgin, Pinar (2010) The "Western-centrism" of Security Studies: "Blind Spot" or Constitutive Practice? *Security Dialogue* 41(6): 615–622.

Bilgin, Pinar (2016) "Contrapuntal Reading" as a Method, an Ethos, and a Metaphor for Global IR. *International Studies Review* 18(1): 1–13.

Bleiker, Roland (2001) Identity and Security in Korea. *The Pacific Review* 14(1): 121–148.

Bloom, William (1993) *Personal Identity, National Identity, and International Relations*. Cambridge: Cambridge University Press.

Brady, Henry E. and David Collier (eds) (2010) *Rethinking Social Inquiry: Diverse Tools, Shared Standards*, 2nd edition. Lanham, MD: Rowman & Littlefield.

Braspenning, Thierry and Stéphane J. Baele (2010) The Third Debate and Postpositivism. In R. Denemark (ed.) *International Studies Encyclopedia*. Chichester: Blackwell. DOI: 10.1111/b.9781444336597.2010.x.

Brecher, Michael and Frank Harvey (eds) (2002) *Millennial Reflections on International Studies*. Ann Arbor, MI: University of Michigan Press.

Breslin, Shaun (2007) Theorising East Asian Regionalism(s): New Regionalism and Asia's Future(s). In Melissa Curley and Nicholas Thomas (eds) *Advancing East Asian Regionalism*. London: Routledge, 26–51.

Bryant, Christopher G. A. (1985) *Positivism in Social Theory and Research*. London: Palgrave Macmillan.

Buzan, Barry (2016) Could IR Be Different? *International Studies Review* 18(1): 155–157.

Buzan, Barry and Richard Little (2001) Why International Relations has Failed as an Intellectual Project and What to Do about It. *Millennium: Journal of International Studies* 30(1): 19–31.

Caldwell, Bruce J. (2003) *Beyond Positivism: Economic Methodology in the Twentieth Century*, 2nd edition. London: Routledge.

Callahan, William A. (2001) China and the Globalisation of IR Theory: Discussion of Building International Relations Theory with Chinese Characteristics. *Journal of Contemporary China* 10(26): 75–88.

Callahan, William A. (2008) Chinese Visions of World Order: Post-hegemonic or a New Hegemony. *International Studies Review* 10(4): 749–761.

Campbell, David (1992) *Writing Security: United States Foreign Policy and Politics of Identity*. Manchester: Manchester University Press.

Campbell, David (2013) Poststructuralism. In Tim Dunne, Milja Kurki, and Steve Smith (eds) *International Relations Theories: Discipline and Diversity*, 3rd edition. Oxford: Oxford University Press, 223–246.

Carvalho, Benjaminde, Halvard Leira, and John M. Hobson (2011) The Big Bangs of IR: The Myths that Your Teachers Still Tell You about 1648 and 1919. *Millennium: Journal of International Studies* 39(3): 735–758.

Checkel, Jeffrey T. (2013) Theoretical Pluralism in IR: Possibilities and Limits. In Walter Carlsnaes, Thomas Risse, and Beth A. Simmons (eds) *Handbook of International Relations*, 2nd edition. London: SAGE Publications, 220–241.

Chen, Ching-Chang (2011) The Absence of Non-Western IR Theory in Asia Reconsidered. *International Relations of the Asia-Pacific* 11(1): 1–23.

Chen, Ching-Chang (2012) The Im/possibility of Building Indigenous Theories in a Hegemonic Discipline: The Case of Japanese International Relations. *Asian Perspective* 36(3): 463–492.

Cho, Young Chul (2015) Colonialism and Imperialism in the Quest for a Universalist Korean-style International Relations Theory. *Cambridge Review of International Affairs* 28(4): 680–700.

Choe, Hyun (2006) National Identity and Citizenship in the People's Republic of China and the Republic of Korea. *Journal of Historical Sociology* 19(1): 84–118.

Choi, Jong Kun (2008) Theorizing East Asian International Relations in Korea. *Asian Perspective* 32(1): 193–216.

Chun, Chaesung (2007) Future Tasks for Developing the Field of International Relations in South Korea. *Korean Journal of International Relations* 46: 227–249 (in Korean).

Chun, Chaesung and Kun Young Park (2002) Reflections on International Relations Theories in Korea: In Search of Alternatives. *Korean Journal of International Relations* 42(4): 7–26 (in Korean).

Cohen, Ira J. (1989) *Structuration Theory: Anthony Giddens and the Constitution of Social Life*. Basingstoke: Palgrave Macmillan.

Collier, David and Colin Elman (2008) Qualitative and Multimethod Research: Organizations, Publication, and Reflections on Integration. In Janet M. Box-Steffensmeier, Henry Brady, and David Collier (eds) *Oxford Handbook of Political Methodology*. Oxford: Oxford University Press, 779–795.

Cornut, Jeremie (2015) Analytic Eclecticism in Practice: A Method for Combining International Relations Theories. *International Studies Perspectives* 16(1): 50–66.

Cox, Robert W. (1981) Social Forces, States and World Orders: Beyond International Relations Theory. *Millenium: Journal of International Studies* 10(2): 126–155.

Cox, Robert W. (1986) Social Forces, States and World Orders: Beyond International Relations Theory. In Robert O. Keohane (ed.) *Neorealism and Its Critics*. New York: Columbia University Press, 204–254.

Creutzfeldt, B. (2012) Theory Talk #51: Yan Xuetong on Chinese Realism, the Tsinghua School of International Relations, and the Impossibility of Harmony. *Theory Talks*, 28 November. Available at: www.theory-talks.org/2012/11/theory-talk-51.html (accessed 8 February, 2017).

Devetak, Richard (2014) A Rival Enlightenment? Critical International Theory in Historical Mode. *International Theory* 6(3): 417–422.

Dunne, Tim, Lene Hansen, and Colin Wight (2013a) The End of International Relations Theory? *European Journal of International Relations* 19(3): 405–425.

Dunne, Tim, Milja Kurki, and Steve Smith (2013b) *International Relations Theories: Discipline and Diversity*, 3rd edition. Oxford: Oxford University Press.

Dyson, Stephen Benedict and Thomas Preston (2006) Individual Characteristics of Political Leaders and the Use of Analogy in Foreign Policy Decision Making. *Political Psychology* 27(2): 265–288.

EAI (East Asia Institute) (2014). The 2nd Joint Korea-Japan Public Opinion Poll: Analysis Report on Comparative Data. *EIA*, 13 August. Available at: http://m.eai.or.kr/eng/sub03_04_02.asp?bytag=n&catcode=+&code=eng_report&idx=13207&page=3 (accessed 11 December, 2016).

Eckert, Carter J. (1991) *Offspring of Empire: The Kochang Kims and the Colonial Origins of Korean Capitalism*. Seattle: University of Washington Press.

Edkins, Jenny (2003) *Trauma and the Memory of Politics*. Cambridge: Cambridge University Press.

Eun, Yong-Soo (2012) Why and How Should We Go for a Multicausal Analysis in the Study of Foreign Policy? (Meta-)theoretical Rationales and Methodological Rules. *Review of International Studies* 38(4): 763–783.

Eun, Yong-Soo (2016) *Pluralism and Engagement in the Discipline of International Relations*. London: Palgrave Macmillan.

Ferguson, Yale H. (2015) Diversity in IR Theory: Pluralism as an Opportunity for Understanding Global Politics. *International Studies Perspectives* 16(1): 3–12.

Friedberg, Aron (2005) The Future of U.S.-China Relations: Is Conflict Inevitable? *International Security* 30(2): 7–45.

Gellner, Ernest (1983) *Muslim Society*. Cambridge: Cambridge University Press.

George, Alexander L. (1969) The "Operational Code": A Neglected Approach to the Study of Political Leaders and Decision-making. *International Studies Quarterly* 13(2): 190–222.

George, Alexander L. and Andrew Bennett (2005) *Case Studies and Theory Development in the Social Sciences.* Cambridge, MA: MIT Press.

George, Jim (1989) International Relations and the Search for Thinking Space: Another View of the Third Debate. *International Studies Quarterly* 33(3): 269–279.

Giddens, Anthony (1974) *Positivism and Sociology.* London: Heinemann Educational Books.

Giddens, Anthony (1979) *Central Problems in Social Theory: Action, Structure and Contradiction in Social Analysis.* California: University of California Press.

Glosserman, Brad and Scott A. Snyder (2015) *The Japan-South Korea Identity Clash: East Asian Security and the United States.* New York: Columbia University Press.

Gramsci, Antonio (1971) *Selections from the Prison Notebooks.* New York: International Publishers.

Guibernau, Montserrat (2004) Anthony D. Smith on Nations and National Identity: A Critical Assessment. *Nations and Nationalism* 10(1–2): 125–141.

Guzzini, Stefano (2005) The Concept of Power: A Constructivist Analysis. *Millennium: Journal of International Studies* 33(3): 495–521.

Guzzini, Stefano (2013) The Ends of International Relations Theory: Stages of Reflexivity and Modes of Theorizing. *European Journal of International Relations* 19(3): 521–541.

Guzzini, Stefano and Anna Leander (eds) (2006) *Constructivism and International Relations: Alexander Wendt and his Critics.* New York: Routledge.

Hagmann, Jonas and Thomas J. Biersteker (2014) Beyond the Published Discipline: Toward a Critical Pedagogy of International Studies. *European Journal of International Relations* 20(2): 291–315.

Hagström, Linus and Gustafsson Karl (2015) Japan and Identity Change: Why It Matters in International Relations. *The Pacific Review* 28(1): 1–22.

Hahm, Taik-young (2008) Theory and History in "Korean" International Relations Theories. *Korea and World Politics* 22(4): 1–40.

Hall, Ian (2009) What Causes What: The Ontologies of Critical Realism. *International Studies Review* 11(4): 629–630.

Hall, Todd and Andrew Ross (2015) Affective Politics after 9/11. *International Organization* 69(4): 847–879.

Hamati-Ataya, Inanna (2013) Reflectivity, Reflexivity, Reflexivism: IR's "Reflexive Turn" – and Beyond. *European Journal of International Relations* 19(4): 669–694.

Hamati-Ataya, Inanna (2014) Transcending Objectivism, Subjectivism, and the Knowledge In-between: The Subject in/of "Strong Reflexivity." *Review of International Studies* 40(1): 153–175.

Hansen, Lene (2006) *Security as Practice: Discourse Analysis and the Bosnian War.* London: Routledge.

Harvey, Frank and Joel Cobb (2003) Multiple Dialogues, Layered Syntheses, and the Limits of Expansive Cumulation. *International Studies Review* 5(1): 144–147.

Hellmann, Gunther (2003) Are Dialogue and Synthesis Possible in International Relations? *International Studies Review* 5(1): 123–153.

Hellmann, Gunther (2014) Methodological Transnationalism – Europe's Offering to Global IR? *European Review of International Studies* 1(1): 25–37.

Herbst, Jeffrey (2000) *States and Power in Africa: Comparative Lessons in Authority and Control.* Princeton, NJ: Princeton University Press.

Hobson, John M. (2012) *The Eurocentric Conception of World Politics: Western International Theory, 1760–2010.* New York: Cambridge University Press.

Hollis, Martin (2002) *The Philosophy of Social Science: An Introduction.* Cambridge: Cambridge University Press.

Hollis, Martin and Steve Smith (1990) *Explaining and Understanding International Relations.* Oxford: Oxford University Press.

Holsti, Ole R. (1962) The Belief System and National Images: A Case Study. *Journal of Conflict Resolution* 6(3): 244–252.

Holsti, Ole R. (1967) Cognitive Dynamics and Images of the Enemy. *Journal of International Affairs* 21(1): 16–39.

Hong, Seongmin (ed.) (2008) *Knowledge and International Politics: Political Power Permeated in Scholarship.* Pajoo: Hanul (in Korean).

Hopf, Ted (1998) The Promise of Constructivism in International Relations Theory. *International Security* 23(1): 171–200.

Horesh, Niv (2013) In Search of the "China Model": Historic Continuity vs. Imagined History in Yan Xuetong's Thought. *China Report* 49(3): 337–355.

Hudson, Valerie M. (2007) *Foreign Policy Analysis: Classic and Contemporary Theory.* Boulder, CO: Rowman & Littlefield.

Hurrell, Andrew (2016) Beyond Critique: How to Study Global IR? *International Studies Review* 18(1): 149–151.

Hutchings, Kimberly (2011) Dialogue between Whom? The Role of the West/Non-West Distinction in Promoting Global Dialogue in IR. *Millennium: Journal of International Studies* 39(3) 639–647.

Hutchison, Emma (2010) Trauma and the Politics of Emotions: Constituting Identity, Security and Community after the Bali Bombing. *International Relations* 24(1): 65–86.

Ikeda, Josuke (2008) *Japanese Vision of International Society: A Historical Exploration.* Presented at the 49th Annual Convention of the International Studies Association, San Francisco, 26 March.

Ikeda, Josuke (2011) The "Westfailure" Problem in International Relations Theory. In Shiro Sato, Josuke Ikeda, Ching-Chang Chen, and Young Chul Cho (eds) *Re-examination of "Non-Western" International Relations Theories.* Kyoto: Kyoto University, 12–41.

Ikenberry, G. John (2009) Liberalism in a Realist World: International Relations as an American Scholarly Tradition. *International Studies* 46(1): 203–219.

Inoguchi, Takashi (2007) Are there any Theories of International Relations in Japan? *International Relations of the Asia-Pacific* 7(3): 369–390.

Jackson, Patrick (2011) *The Conduct of Inquiry in International Relations: Philosophy of Science and Its Implications for the Study of World Politics.* London: Routledge.

Jackson, Patrick (2015) Fear of Relativism. *International Studies Perspectives* 16(1): 13–22.

Johnston, Alastair Iain (2012) What (if Anything) Does East Asia Tell Us about International Relations Theory? *Annual Review of Political Science* 15: 53–78.

Joseph, Jonathan (2007) Philosophy in International Relations: A Scientific Realist Approach. *Millennium: Journal of International Studies* 35(2): 345–359.

Joseph, Jonathan and Colin Wight (eds) (2010) *Scientific Realism and International Relations.* Basingstoke: Palgrave Macmillan.

Kang, David C. (2003) Getting Asia Wrong: The Need for New Analytical Frameworks. *International Security* 27(4): 57–85.

Kang, David C. (2010) *East Asia before the West: Five Centuries of Trade and Tribute.* New York: Columbia University Press.

Katzenstein, Peter J. (1997) Introduction: Asian Regionalism in Comparative Perspective. In Peter J. Katzenstein and Takashi Shiraishi (eds) *Network Power: Japan and Asia.* Ithaca, NY: Cornell University Press, 1–44.

Katzenstein, Peter J. and Nobuo Okawara (2001/2002) Japan, Asian-Pacific Security, and the Case for Analytical Eclecticism. *International Security* 26(3): 153–185.

Keohane, Robert O. (1988) International Institutions: Two approaches. *International Studies Quarterly* 32(4): 379–396.

Kim, Mi Kyung (ed.) (2015) *Routledge Handbook of Memory and Reconciliation in East Asia.* Abingdon, UK: Routledge.

Kim, Sung Bae (2011) *Identity Prevails in the End: North Korea's Nuclear Threat and South Korea's Response in 2006.* EAI Asia Security Initiative Working Paper 18. Seoul: East Asia Institute.

Kim, Sung Hwan (2012) Interview with the Associated Press. *Yonhap News.* Available at: www.yonhapnews.co.kr/bulletin/2012/09/28/0200000000AKR2 0120928006800072.HTML (accessed 30 November 2016).

King, Gary, Robert O. Keohane, and Sidney Verba (1994) *Designing Social Inquiry: Scientific Inference in Qualitative Research.* Princeton, NJ: Princeton University Press.

Kingston, Jeff (2015) *Asian Nationalisms Reconsidered.* Abingdon, UK: Routledge.

Klingner, Bruce (2008) Lee, Bush Affirm Strong Bilateral Partnership. *The Heitage Foundation.* www.heritage.org/asia/commentary/lee-bush-affirm-strong-bilateral-partnership (accessed 1 September, 2017).

Koh, Byung Chul (1994) A Comparison of Unification Policies. In Young W. Kihl (ed.) *Korea and the World: Beyond the Cold War.* Boulder, CO: Westview Press, 153–166.

Kort, Wafa and Jamel Eddine Gharbi (2013) Structuration Theory amid Negative and Positive Criticism. *International Journal of Business and Social Research* 3(5): 92–104.

Kratochwil, Friedrich (2003) The Monologue of "Science." *International Studies Review* 5(1): 124–128.

Kristensen, Peter M. (2015) Revisiting the "American Social Science": Mapping the Geography of International Relations. *International Studies Perspectives* 16(3): 246–269.

Kristensen, Peter M. and Ras T. Nielsen (2013) Constructing a Chinese International Relations Theory: A Sociological Approach to Intellectual Innovation. *International Political Sociology* 7(1): 19–40.

Kuhn, Thomas (1962) *The Structure of Scientific Revolutions*. Chicago, IL: University of Chicago Press.

Kuhn, Thomas (1970) Reflections on My Critics. In Imre Lakatos and Alan Musgrave (eds) *Criticism and the Growth of Knowledge*. Cambridge: Cambridge University Press, 231–278.

Kurki, Milja (2007) Critical Realism and Causal Analysis in International Relations. *Millennium: Journal of International Studies* 35(2): 361–378.

Kurki, Milja (2008) *Causation in International Relations*. Cambridge: Cambridge University Press.

Kurki, Milja (2015) Stretching Situated Knowledge: From Standpoint Epistemology to Cosmology and Back Again. *Millennium: Journal of International Studies* 43(3): 779–797.

Kurki, Milja and Colin Wight (2013) International Relations and Social Science. In Tim Dunne, Milja Kurki, and Steve Smith (eds) *International Relations Theories: Discipline and Diversity*. Oxford: Oxford University Press, 14–35.

Kwak, Jun-Hyeok and Melissa Nobles (eds) (2013) *Inherited Responsibility and Historical Reconciliation in East Asia*. Abingdon, UK: Routledge.

Lake, David (2011) Why "Isms" are Evil: Theory, Epistemology, and Academic Sects as Impediments to Understanding and Progress. *International Studies Quarterly* 55(2): 465–480.

Lake, David (2013) Theory is Dead, Long Live Theory: The End of the Great Debates and the Rise of Eclecticism. *European Journal of International Relations* 19(3): 567–587.

Lake, David (2016) White Man's IR: An Intellectual Confession. *Perspectives on Politics* 14(4): 1112–1122.

Lapid, Yosef (1989) The Third Debate: On the Prospects of International Theory in a Post-positivist Era. *International Studies Quarterly* 33(3): 235–254.

Lapid, Yosef (2003) Through Dialogue to Engaged Pluralism: The Unfinished Business of the Third Debate. *International Studies Review* 5(1): 128–131.

Laudan, Larry (1996) *Beyond Positivism and Relativism: Theory, Method and Evidence*. Boulder, CO: Westview Press.

Lebow, Richard Ned (2011) Philosophy and International Relations. *International Affairs* 87(5): 1219–1228.

Lee, Myung Bak (2010a) President Lee's Address for the 60th Anniversary of the Korean War, 25 June, *President Lee Myung Bak Speeches*. Seoul: CHEONG WA DAE. The Office of President.

Lee, Myung Bak (2010b) Speech on 65th Anniversary of National Liberation, 15 August, *President Lee Myung Bak Speeches*. Seoul: CHEONG WA DAE. The Office of President.

Lee, Myung Bak (2012) The Way for the North to Survive is to Voluntarily Dismantle its Nuclear Weapons and to Cooperate with the International Community through Reform and Open-door Policies, 16 April, *President Lee Myung Bak Speeches*. Seoul: CHEONG WA DAE. The Office of President.

Lee, Myung Bak (2013) *President's Time*. Seoul: RH Korea.

Lee, Nae Young and Han-Wool Jeong (2010) *The Impact of North Korea's Artillery Strike on Public Opinion in South Korea*. EAI Issue Briefing on Public Opinion. Seoul: East Asia Institute. Available at: www.eai.or.kr/data/bbs/eng_report/201101281811046.pdf (accessed 30 November, 2016).

Liang, Shoude (1994) International Politics with "Chinese Characteristics." *Studies of International Politics* 1(1): 15–21.

Ling, Lily H. M. (2013) Worlds Beyond Westphalia: Daoist Dialectics and the "China Threat." *Review of International Studies* 39(3): 549–568.

Ling, Lily H. M. (2014) *The Dao of World Politics: Towards a Post-Westphalian, Worldist International Relations*. London: Routledge.

Lipson, Michael, Daniel Maliniak, Amy Oakes, Susan Peterson, and Micheal Tierney (2007) Divided Discipline? Comparing Views of U.S. and Canadian IR scholars. *International Journal* 62(2): 327–343.

Little, Richard (1996) The Growing Relevance of Pluralism? In Steve Smith, Ken Booth, and Marysia Zalewski (eds) *International Theory: Positivism and Beyond*. Cambridge: Cambridge University Press, 66–86.

Little, Richard and Michael Smith (eds) (2006) *Perspectives on World Politics*. London: Routledge.

Lynch, Cecelia (2008) Reflexivity in Research on Civil Society: Constructivist Perspectives. *International Studies Review* 10(4): 708–721.

McCormick, James M. (1992) *American Foreign Policy and Process*. Itasca, IL: F. E. Peacock Publishers.

McNamara, Kathleen R. (2009) Of Intellectual Monocultures and the Study of IPE. *Review of International Political Economy* 16(1): 72–84.

Maliniak, Daniel, AmyOakes, SusanPeterson, and Michael J. Tierney (2011) International Relations in the US Academy. *International Studies Quarterly* 55(2): 437–464.

Maliniak, Daniel, Susan Peterson, and Michael J. Tierney (2012) *TRIP Around the World: Teaching, Research, and Policy Views of International Relations Faculty in 20 Countries*. Williamsburg, VA: Teaching, Research, and International Policy Project, The Institute for the Theory and Practice of International Relations, The College of William and Mary. www.wm.edu/offices/itpir/_documents/trip/trip_around_the_world_2011.pdf (accessed September 1, 2017).

Marsh, David and Paul Furlong (2002) A Skin not a Sweater: Ontology and Epistemology in Political Science. In David Marsh and Gerry Stoker (eds) *Theory and Methods in Political Science*. New York: Palgrave Macmillan, 21–35.

Matthews, Elizabeth G. and Rhonda L. Callaway (2015) Where Have All the Theories Gone? Teaching Theory in Introductory Courses in International Relations. *International Studies Perspectives* 16(2): 190–209.

Mead, Lawrence (2010) Scholasticism in Political Science. *Perspectives on Politics* 8(2): 453–464.

Mearsheimer, John (2016) Benign Hegemony. *International Studies Review* 18(1): 147–149.

Mearsheimer, John J. and Stephen M. Walt (2013) Leaving Theory Behind: Why Simplistic Hypothesis Testing is Bad for IR. *European Journal of International Relations* 19(3): 427–457.

Mercer, Jonathan (2014) Feeling like a State: Social Emotion and Identity. *International Theory* 6(3): 515–535.

Milliken, Jennifer (1999) The Study of Discourse in International Relations: A Critique of Research and Methods. *European Journal of International Relations* 5(2): 225–254.

Min, Byoung Won (2007) International Relations Theories and Korea: A Critical Review and Some Suggestions. *Korean Journal of International Relations* 46: 37–66 (in Korean).

Min, Byoung Won (2016) *Not So Much Universal? Passions for Indigenous International Theories in South Korea.* Paper presented at the 60th Anniversary of the Korean Association of International Studies.

Monteiro, Nuno and Keven G. Ruby (2009) IR and the False Promise of Philosophical Foundations. *International Theory* 1(1): 15–48.

Nau, Henry R. (2015) *Perspectives on International Relations: Power, Institutions, and Ideas.* London: Sage Publications.

Neumann, Iver B. (2014) International Relations as a Social Science. *Millennium: Journal of International Studies* 43(1): 330–350.

Olsen, Edward (2008) Korean Nationalism in a Divided Nation: Challenges to US Policy. *Pacific Focus* 23(1): 4–21.

Oren, Ido (2016) A Sociological Analysis of the Decline of American IR Theory. *International Studies Review* 18(4): 571–596.

Park, Chan Wook (2005) Political Science in Korea. *Political Science in Asia* 1(1): 63–86.

Pasha, Mustapha Kamal (2011) Western Nihilism and Dialogue: Prelude to an Uncanny Encounter in International Relations. *Millennium: Journal of International Studies* 39(3): 683–699.

Patomäki, Heikki (2002) *After International Relations: Critical Realism and the (Re)Construction of World Politics.* London: Routledge.

Patomäki, Heikki (2007) Back to the Kantian Idea for a Universal History? Overcoming Eurocentric Accounts of the International Problematic. *Millennium: Journal of International Studies* 35(3): 575–595.

Paul, T. V. (ed.) (2016) *Accommodating Rising Powers: Past, Present and Future.* New York: Cambridge University Press.

Pennebaker, James, Dario Paez, and Bernard Rim (2013) *Collective Memory of Political Events: Social Psychological Perspectives.* New York: Psychology Press.

Poole, Marshall Scott and Gerardine DeSanctis (2004) Structuration Theory in Information Systems Research: Methods and Controversies. In M. E. Whitman and A. Woszcynski (eds) *Handbook of Information Systems Research.* Hershey, PA: Idea Group Publishing, 206–249.

Poole, Ross (1999) *Nation and Identity.* London: Routledge.

Pouliot, Vincent (2007) "Sobjectivism": Toward a Constructivist Methodology. *International Studies Quarterly* 51(2): 359–384.

Qin, Yaqing (2007) Why Is There No Chinese International Relations Theory? *International Relations of the Asia-Pacific* 7(3): 313–340.

Qin, Yaqing (2011) Development of International Relations Theory in China: Progress through Debates. *International Relations of the Asia-Pacific* 11(2): 231–257.

Qin, Yaqing (2016) A Relational Theory of World Politics. *International Studies Review* 18(1): 33–47.

Rengger, Nicholas (2015) Pluralism in International Relations Theory: Three Questions. *International Studies Perspectives* 16(1): 32–39.

Renshon, Jonathan (2008) Stability and Change in Belief Systems: The Operational Code of George W. Bush From Governor to Second Term President. *Journal of Conflict Resolution* 52(6): 820–849.

Reus-Smit, Christian (2013) Beyond Metatheory? *European Journal of International Relations* 19(3): 589–608.

Rivas, Jorge (2010) Realism. For Real this Time: Scientific Realism is not a Compromise between Positivism and Interpretivism. In Jonathan Joseph and Colin Wight (eds) *Scientific Realism and International Relations.* Basingstoke: Palgrave Macmillan, 203–227.

Roh, Moo-hyun (2006a) Speeches on March First Independence Movement Day Address, March 1. *President Roh Moo-hyun Speeches.* Seoul: CHEONWA DEA. The Office of President.

Roh, Moo-hyun (2006b) Letters on South Korea-Japan Relations. *President Roh Moo-hyun Speeches.* Seoul: CHEONWA DEA. The Office of President.

Rozman, Gilbert (ed.) (2012) *East Asian National Identities: Common Roots and Chinese Exceptionalism.* Washington, DC: Wilson Center.

Samuels, Warren J. (ed.) (1980) *The Methodology of Economic Thought: Critical Papers from the Journal of Economic Thought.* New Brunswick, NJ: Transaction Books.

Samuels, Warren J. (ed.) (1990) *Economics as Discourse: An Analysis of the Language of Economists.* Boston: Kluwer Academic.

Sato, Shiro (2011) The IR Discipline would Discipline Asian Studies. In Shiro Sato, Ikeda Josuke, Ching-Chan Chen, and Young Chul Cho (eds) *Re-Examination of "Non-Western" International Relations Theories.* Kyoto: Kyoto University, 1–11.

Schafer, Mark and Stephen G. Walker (2006) *Beliefs and Leadership in World Politics: Methods and Applications of Operational Code Analysis.* New York: Palgrave.

Schmidt, Brian (2008) International Relations Theory: Hegemony or Pluralism? *Millennium: Journal of International Studies* 36(2): 105–114.

Shambaugh, David (2011) International Relations Studies in China: History, Trends, and Prospects. *International Relations of the Asia-Pacific* 11(3): 339–372.

Shin, Gi-Wook (2015) National Identities, Historical Memories, and Reconciliation in Northeast Asia. In Gilbert Rozman (ed.) *Asia's Alliance Triangle*. Basingstoke, UK: Palgrave Macmillan, 189–202.

Shin, Gi-Wook and Paul Yunsik Chang (2004) The Politics of Nationalism in U.S.-Korean Relations. *Asian Perspective* 28(3): 119–145.

Shin, Gi-Wook, James Freda, and Gihong Yi (1999) The Politics of Ethnic Nationalism in Divided Korea. *Nations and Nationalism* 5(4): 465–484.

Sil, Rudra and Peter J. Katzenstein (2010) Analytical Eclecticism in the Study of World Politics: Reconfiguring Problems and Mechanisms across Research Traditions. *Perspectives on Politics* 8(2): 411–423.

Sil, Rudra and Peter J. Katzenstein (2011) De-centering, not Discarding the "Isms": Some Friendly Amendments. *International Studies Quarterly* 55(2): 481–485.

Sjoberg, Laura (2015) What's Lost in Translation? Neopositivism and Critical Research Interests. *Millennium: Journal of International Studies* 43(3): 1007–1010.

Sjoberg, Laura and Kevin Knudson (2017) Theoretical Geometry, Critical Theory, and Concept Spaces in IR. In J. Samuel Barkin and Laura Sjoberg (eds) *Interpretive Quantification: Methodological Explorations for Critical and Constructivist IR*. Ann Arbor, MI: University of Michigan Press, 196–223.

Sjoberg, Laura and Jeffrey Horowitz (2013) Quantitative Methods in Critical Security Studies. In Laura J. Shepherd (ed.) *Critical Approaches to Security: Theories and Methods*. New York: Routledge, 103–117.

Smith, Anthony (1986) *The Ethnic Origins of Nations*. Oxford: Basic Blackwell.

Smith, Anthony (1991) *National Identity*. Reno, NV: University of Nevada Press.

Smith, Anthony (1998) *Nationalism and Modernism: A Critical Survey of Recent Theories of Nation and Nationalism*. London: Routledge.

Smith, Steve (1987) Paradigm Dominance in International Relations: The Development of International Relations as a Social Science. *Millennium: Journal of International Studies* 16(2): 189–206.

Smith, Steve (1996) Positivism and Beyond. In Steve Smith, Ken Booth, and Marysia Zalewski (eds) *International Theory: Positivism and Beyond*. Cambridge: Cambridge University Press, 11–44.

Smith, Steve (2002) Alternative and Critical Perspectives. In Michael Brecher and Frank P. Harvey (eds) *Millennial Reflections on International Studies*. Ann Arbor, MI: University of Michigan Press, 195–208.

Smith, Steve (2003) Dialogue and the Reinforcement of Orthodoxy in International Relations. *International Studies Review* 5(1): 141–143.

Smith, Steve, Ken Booth, and Marysia Zalewski (eds) (1996) *International Theory: Positivism and Beyond*. Cambridge: Cambridge University Press.

Song, Xinning (2001) Building International Relations Theory with Chinese Characteristics. *Journal of Contemporary China* 10(26): 61–74.

Suganami, Hidemi (2013) Meta-Jackson: Rethinking Patrick Thaddeus Jackson's Conduct of Inquiry. *Millennium: Journal of International Studies* 41(2): 248–269.

Sylvester, Christine (2013) The Elusive Arts of Reflexivity in the "Sciences" of International Relations. *Millennium: Journal of International Studies* 41(2): 309–325.

Thrift, Nigel (1985) Flies and Germs: A Geography of Knowledge. In Derek Gregory and John Urry (eds) *Social Relations and Spatial Structure.* Basingstoke, UK: Palgrave Macmillan, 366–403.

Tickner, Arlene B. (2013) Core, Periphery and (Neo)Imperialist International Relations. *European Journal of International Relations* 19(3): 627–646.

Tickner, Arlene B. and Ole Wæver (eds) (2009) *International Relations Scholarship around the World.* New York: Routledge.

Tickner, J. Ann (2005) So What Is Your Research Program? Some Feminist Answers to International Relations Methodological Questions? *International Studies Quarterly* 49(1): 1–22.

Tickner, J. Ann (2011) Dealing with Difference: Problems and Possibilities for Dialogue in International Relations. *Millennium: Journal of International Studies* 39(3): 607–618. Tickner, J. Ann (2016) Knowledge Is Power: Challenging IR's Eurocentric Narrative. *International Studies Review* 18(1): 157–159.

Turton, Helen Louise (2016) *International Relations and American Dominance: A Diverse Discipline.* New York: Routledge.

van der Ree, Gerard (2013) The Politics of Scientific Representation in International Relations. *Millennium: Journal of International Studies* 42(1): 24–44.

van der Ree, Gerard (2014) Saving the Discipline: Plurality, Social Capital, and the Sociology of IR Theorizing. *International Political Sociology* 8(2): 218–233.

Van Fraassen, Bas C. (1980) *The Scientific Image.* Oxford: Oxford University Press.

Vertzberger, Yaacov I. (2005) The Practice and Power of Collective Memory. *International Studies Review* 7(3): 117–121.

Wæver, Ole (1996) The Rise and Fall of the Inter-paradigm Debate. In Steve Smith, Ken Booth, and Marysia Zalewski (eds) *International Theory: Positivism and Beyond.* Cambridge: Cambridge University Press, 149–185.

Wæver, Ole (1998) The Sociology of a Not So International Discipline: American and European Developments in International Relations. *International Organization* 52(4): 687–727.

Wæver, Ole (2007) Still a Discipline after All These Debates? In Tim Dunne, Milja Kurki, and Steve Smith (eds) *International Relations Theories: Discipline and Diversity.* Oxford: Oxford University Press, 297–318.

Walt, Stephen M. (2011) Is IR Still "an American Social Science"? *Foreign Policy.* Available at: www.foreignpolicy.com/posts/2011/06/06/is_ir_still_an_american_social_science (accessed 2 February, 2017).

Wan, Ming (2012) Introduction: Chinese Traditions in International Relations. *Journal of Chinese Political Science* 17(2): 105–109.

Wang, Qingxin K. and Mark Blyth (2013) Constructivism and the Study of International Political Economy in China. *Review of International Political Economy* 20(6): 1276–1299.

Wang, Yuan-kang (2011) *Harmony and War: Confucian Culture and Chinese Power Politics*. New York: Columbia University Press.

Wang, Yuan-kang (2013) Explaining the Tribute System: Power, Confucianism, and War in Medieval East Asia. *Journal of East Asian Studies* 13(2): 207–232.

Wang, Zheng (2013) Perception Gaps, Identity Clashes. In T. Arai, S. Goto, and Z. Wang (eds) *Clash of National Identities: China, Japan and the China Sea Territorial Dispute*. Washington, DC: Wilson Center, 9–18.

Weber, Max (1968) *Economy and Society*. New York: Bedminster Press.

Weiner, Michael (1997) *Japan's Minorities: The Illusion of Homogeneity*. London: Routledge.

Wemheuer-Vogelaar, Wiebke, Nicholas J. Bell, Mariana Navarrete Morales, and Michael J. Tierney (2016) The IR of the Beholder: Examining Global IR Using the 2014 TRIP Survey. *International Studies Review* 18(1): 16–32.

Wendt, Alexander (1994) Collective Identity Formation and the International State. *American Political Science Review* 88(2): 384–396.

Wendt, Alexander (1995) Constructing International Politics. *International Security* 20(1): 71–81.

Wendt, Alexander (1999) *Social Theory of International Politics*. Cambridge: Cambridge University Press.

Wendt, Alexander (2015) *Quantum Mind and Social Science*. Cambridge: Cambridge University Press.

Wight, Colin (2002) Philosophy of Social Science and International Relations. In Walter Carlsnaes, Thomas Risse, and Beth A. Simmons (eds) *Handbook of International Relations*. London: Sage, 23–51.

Wight, Colin (2006) *Agents, Structures and International Relations*. Cambridge: Cambridge University Press.

Wight, Colin (2013) The Dualistic Grounding of Monism: Science, Pluralism and Typological Truncation. *Millennium: Journal of International Studies* 41(2): 326–345.

Xuetong, Yan (2011) *Ancient Chinese Thought, Modern Chinese Power*. Princeton, NJ: Princeton University Press.

Yamamoto, Kazuya (2011) International Relations Studies and Theories in Japan: A Trajectory Shaped by War, Pacifism, and Globalization. *International Relations of the Asia-Pacific* 11(2): 259–278.

Yanow, Dvora and Peregrine Schwartz-Shea (2010) Perestroika Ten Years After: Reflections on Methodological Diversity. *PS: Political Science and Politics* 43(4): 741–745.

Young, Michael D. and Mark Schafer (1998) Is There Method in Our Madness? Ways of Assessing Cognition in International Relations. *Mershon International Studies Review* 42(1): 63–96.

Yu, Jinseog and Kun Young Park (2008) Study of International Relations in Korea: Reality and Search for an Alternative. *Journal of Asia–Pacific Studies* 15(1): 57–71 (in Korean).

Zahran, Geraldo and Leonardo Ramos (2011) From Hegemony to Soft Power: Implications for Conceptual Change. In Inderjeet Parmar and Michael Cox (eds) *Soft Power and US Foreign Policy: Theoretical, Historical and Contemporary Perspectives.* New York: Routledge, 12–31.

Zhang, Feng (2012) The Tsinghua Approach and the Inception of Chinese Theories of International Relations. *Chinese Journal of International Politics* 5(1): 73–102.

Zhao, Tingyang (2009) A Political World Philosophy in Terms of All-under-heaven (Tian-xia). *Diogenes* 56(1): 5–18.

Index

Page numbers in *italics* refer to tables.

pedagogy *see* IR pedagogy
philosophy of science 19–20, 24–5,
41, 42–3, 46
pluralism 7, 46–7; and dialogue
across theoretical and spatial
divides 12–14; extent of 10–12;
"integrative pluralism" 13–14,
54–5, 72; need for 8–10; "pluralist
turn" 25; socio-epistemic issues in
47–52; *see also* diversity
positivism 18–21, 22, 23–5,
40; American IR 27–8, 29,
36–7; Asian IR 43–5;
limitations of 47–8; literature
review 41–3
positivist–post-positivist divide
53–4; Critical Realism in
methodological practice 65–8;
dialogue and engagement 54–65,
71–2
post-positivism; limitations of
41–3, 60–5; marginalisation 25,
45–6, 88; practice 45–7; research
25–36; *see also* reflexive solidarity;
reflexivity

Qin, Yaqing 2–3, 4, 8, 26, 27, 58

"reflectivism" 25
reflexive solidarity 89–93
reflexivity 20–1, 45–6, 57, 63–4; roles
89–91; self- 91–3; "strong
reflexivity" 20, 41–2, 90
"relational theory" 8

science, disciplinary socialization in
48–50
"science question" 24–5, 64
"scientific" claims 22, 24
"scientific methods" 36
"scientific" research 59
self-reflexivity 91–3
Sil, Rudra 9, 22, 54, 62
Sjoberg, Laura 55, 57, 63
Smith, Steve 7, 18–19, 42, 64
solidarity, reflexive 89–93
South Korea; foreign policy actions
towards N Korea and Japan
79–83; national identity 76–9, 83
"strong reflexivity" 20, 41–2, 90

Teaching, Research, and
International Policy (TRIP)
project 10–11, 28
Tickner, J. Ann 1, 7, 26, 30, 37, 62
"title of science"/"science question"
24–5, 64

universality 5, 49–50

Wæver, Ole 25, 26, 35, 56
Wendt, Alexander 9, 24, 30, 31,
73, 74
Western–non-Western divide and
dialogue 70–2; implications 83–7;
Western-centric IR theory and
indigenous knowledge of East Asia
72–83
Wight, Colin 24, 37, 42, 66

For Product Safety Concerns and Information please contact our EU
representative GPSR@taylorandfrancis.com Taylor & Francis Verlag GmbH,
Kaufingerstraße 24, 80331 München, Germany

Printed and bound by CPI Group (UK) Ltd, Croydon, CR0 4YY
11/04/2025
01843992-0003